TABLE BY THE RIVER

Happy Birthday Tanya!
Anita Gamache

DIETMAR SAWYERE

TABLE BY THE RIVER

Photography by Graeme Gillies

NEW HOLLAND

Contents

On cooking and dining   8

1 The *amuse gueule*   14

2 The first course   34

3 The crustacean course   56

4 The vegetable course   76

5 The fish course   94

6 The soup course   116

7 Poultry and game birds   134

8 Butcher's meat   162

9 Game meat and offal   184

10 Cheese   206

11 Desserts   220

12 Petits four   246

Basic recipes   256

Acknowledgements   268

Index   269

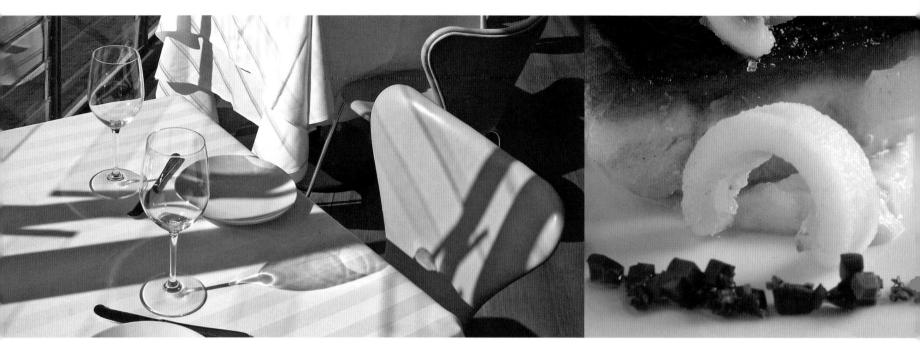

On cooking and dining

Dinner service ... the dining room is dimly lit, warm and inviting. Guests are arriving, ready to celebrate by sharing a meal of fine cuisine and great wines. They are encouraged to take their time, relax and enjoy the moment. No one rushes and time passes easily as one delectable course of the *menu degustation* after another arrives effortlessly at the table. Aside from the animated conversation of some diners, the quickest perceivable movements are those of two pelicans gliding past the windows—no doubt off in search of an evening snack before finding a cosy place to rest for the night.

Upon serving his guests, the commis waiter leaves the table as unobtrusively as he arrived and glides back to the kitchen. He pushes through the large fire-rated doors into another world.

'PICK UP! ... table 22, beef cover one, lamb cover two ... NOW! ... move ... what are you doing? I said I wanted two prawns, one duck, you idiot— not two duck, one prawns! ... Listen to the orders more carefully!' Here the serenity of the restaurant is unknown. This is the battlefield, the lights are bright, the noise incessant, the communication is succinct, brash and often just plain abusive. In this white-tiled, stainless steel-clad room, the chef and his brigade are waging a war against incoming orders.

With temperatures in excess of 40°C (104°F), the brigade of culinary professionals fight like any well-drilled military unit. This is a one of the country's best restaurants, the culinary equivalent of Special Forces! The lethal armory of salamanders, deep-fryers,

scorching hot stoves and boiling pans is their territory. The cooks on each 'partie' are expert in attacking the area in which they work and they do so automatically, firing dishes continuously until the orders begin to retreat or their ammunition—*mise en place*—is exhausted. The chef on the pass fires another barrage of orders; the cooks answer '*Oui!*' The line of fire is continuous, the infernos of the ovens are ablaze, the cooks continue their combat amidst the clang of pots, pans and constant cries. 'More plates.' 'No, the large bowls, quickly!'

Twice a day the battle is waged anew. The enemies are complacency and mediocrity … the fight is constant and difficult as the battle is ever-changing. The chef must inspire his team to refuse mediocrity, defy complacency, fight for perfection, remain enthusiastic and aspire to greatness. Only then can the battle be won!

What of the guests in all this ? They remain in the calm serenity of the dining room, blissfully unaware of the war raging in the kitchen. They reap the spoils of victory from a battle they never knew existed.

The above scene is played out in top restaurant kitchens around the globe on a daily basis by teams of dedicated professionals seeking culinary perfection. Of course, that is unachievable, but the idea of it inspires those who seek it. The main purpose is to make the diners happy. To keep cooking well—striving for that elusive perfection—on a daily basis needs discipline and a passion for what you are doing. Even after all my

years in the kitchen and running restaurants, nothing is more enjoyable than a day spent doing the *mise en place*, setting up for 'service' and wiping down the benches at the end of a day where we have made people happy.

Restaurant cooking at the highest level is not about convenience and it is not about shortcuts. Many of the recipes in this book would be difficult to do in a domestic kitchen, but not impossible. Our lifestyle leans towards instant gratification, but the joy of good cooking is about taking time, showing patience, moving slowly and enjoying the experience—then you may produce something of great beauty and skill.

Writing a cook book is not easy, as I'm a chef who likes to constantly question, evolve and redefine my dishes and techniques. The recipes in this book are a snapshot of what I am cooking as I write it, and even by the time it is published many of the ideas will have morphed into something else. By itself, a recipe has no soul: only when a cook takes that recipe and works with it does it gain a life of its own. I have enjoyed meals at restaurants made by cooks who have passed through my kitchens and often I can recognise the

idea behind a dish because it started life on my stove. One cook may have taken an idea in one direction, whereas I might have developed it in another way altogether. Hopefully, you will take elements of these dishes and make them your own. I have broken each recipe into its component parts to make the transition from my ideas to your creations easier. These recipes are only guidelines, and although they are exact guidelines as they stand, every piece of meat is different, every vegetable, every stove and, more importantly, everyone's taste is different. So by all means copy these recipes and you will achieve good results, but also be inspired by them and you will achieve great ones! … *Amities gourmandises*.

Using the recipes

I am often asked if I enjoy cooking at home and most people are surprised when I answer yes. Cooking at home is very different to producing food in a professional kitchen. Of course, the equipment is different but, most importantly, at home it is usually you cooking by yourself—although the children love to join in and help! In a professional kitchen there are many bodies working on a single dish, with various elements coming from different 'parties' or sections of the kitchen. At home you have to plan

LAMB POT AU FEU

ahead a bit more, especially when attempting a more complicated recipe. Here are a few common threads and general rules that I have not listed in every recipe but apply across the board when cooking:

I season with sea salt—the better quality the better. If you season lightly and often while cooking, at the end you should not need to readjust the seasoning. No weights or measurements are given for seasonings as you should always add these to your taste.

Where butter is listed as an ingredient, I am referring to unsalted butter. Buy the best quality butter you can afford and check the expiry date.

Blanch vegetables in a large pot of rapidly boiling salted water and plunge them into a bowl of ice water as soon as they are ready.

Use fresh herbs unless otherwise stated.

Use the correct equipment for each job listed. When purchasing cooking equipment, buy the best you can. Start with a set of good-quality knives. Good equipment pays dividends over time and makes a significant difference to the quality of a finished dish.

Always purchase ingredients that are in season and the best quality you can find. A restaurant is only as good as the products it uses and the home kitchen is the same. We have a network of suppliers we have worked with over the years—you can do the same by getting to know your butcher and your greengrocer and asking them to source ingredients for you.

And always cook with love and passion, whether it is an important dinner party or breakfast for the kids.

AMUSE GUELE

THE AMUSE QUEUE

On what makes a successful restaurant

Opening and maintaining a restaurant continues to be one of the business world's great gambles. A lot of people who enjoy food, who love cooking and entertaining their friends, think they can open a restaurant—after all 'how hard can it be?' … Well, considering that 75 per cent of new restaurants close within their first three years, obviously it is harder than many people think.

A restaurant is a sum of many parts and each part is vital to the overall effect and its connection with its diners. It is easy to say what causes a restaurant to fail and there is usually a long list of critics and customers who will help the restaurateur by pointing out these shortcomings. But what makes one restaurant succeed over another will always remain a mystery because, like great theatre or a beautiful work of art, it is dependent on so many different elements coming together to please not just one individual but enough people who are willing to patronise the restaurant on a regular basis.

At the budget end of the business, it is easy enough to replicate a success—just look at McDonald's. But when it comes to fine dining, the cookie-cutter approach does not work—that is, assuming you already have one restaurant that is a success. Even the world's greatest chefs and restaurateurs have failures. These days an upmarket restaurant must deliver the complete package—the quality of the food, the location, the décor, the menu, the wine list, the service, the atmosphere and even the aroma of the place—to achieve a synchronicity, a clarity of purpose, a vision that reflects the restaurateur's aspirations. Each diner places different values on each of these items. Once you have been skilled or lucky enough to create a mix that combines all the above criteria and that appeals to a critical mass of diners, then the hard work begins, for you are only as good as your last performance. It is essential, certainly in the early years of a restaurant's life, that its creator is on hand to ensure all the little details of the vision are fulfilled, not just when the staff feel like it but for every customer during every service. Sometimes even when you get all of these elements correct and put in all the hard work, it still fails to fire. Well, as the French so aptly put it, *c'est la vie!*

The role of the *amuse gueule*

The literal translation of the French *amuse gueule* (and of *amuse bouche*, its alternative name) is 'mouth amuser'. The *amuse* usually consists of a single bite-sized portion that is presented by the chef as a taste tickler to get the meal under way.

The *amuse* as a plated dish really came to the fore during the nouvelle cuisine movement of the 1970s and at some point it moved from being an unexpected bonus to being de rigeur in restaurants that had pretensions to being fine dining establishments. The *amuse* implies a certain level of quality and service, which is probably why it is showing up at modestly priced restaurants where the chef is taking his menu and guests seriously and wants them to understand this.

The *amuse* can range from a small bowl of olives right through to a miniature portion of one of the

chef's more elaborate dishes. The style of the *amuse* will tell you a lot about the kitchen and what it is trying to achieve. In the nouvelle kitchens, the *amuse* was a way to set the scene and add a bit more substance to the meagre portions of the era. As it progressed, it became a way to outdo the competition. Still today at top restaurants you will get at least one, and up to four, *amuse* dishes delivered with great pomp and ceremony before you finally get what you ordered.

For me, the *amuse* is a great way to welcome diners to the restaurant, to display some hospitality and give them something to nibble while enjoying their aperitifs. In a more practical sense, it also fills the gap between ordering and the arrival of the first course, which may take time to prepare and cook.

Because the *amuse* is not a full course, it can be light-hearted and provocative. It should explode with flavour and texture, and can be elegant or casual, luxurious or rustic.

The natural extension of the introductory *amuse* is to add further 'taste ticklers' throughout the meal, and we do this with addition of a demitasse of soup before the final savoury course and a small 'pre-dessert' before the finale of dessert. Add to this the canapés to eat while perusing the menu and the petits four with coffee and you have almost enough courses to make a meal in and of themselves!

One final word on the *amuse* and all its cousins served throughout the meal: they are not complimentary, no matter what the waiter says. The price is built into the meal and nothing is more irritating than being given something with the 'compliments of the chef', unless of course it is a bottle of champagne or something else that is truly complimentary.

On the importance of the menu

Menus are a restaurant's best marketing tool. Aside from being an expression of the chef's creativity, they set the tone of the restaurant, creating excitement and the expectation of what is to come.

In its simplest form, the menu is just a piece of paper on which the names of dishes are scribbled by the chef and photocopied. At its most complex, it is a large, leather-bound and tasselled tome of information. Some restaurants are even putting their menus on small electronic screens given to each guest.

The word 'menu' was first recorded back in 1718 in France. The practice of preparing the menu is, of course, much older and prior to 1718 it was known as the *escriteau* or 'bill of fare'. These 'bills of fare' were often more of a guide for the serving staff than for the diners because usually all the dishes were served anyway.

Even though the word 'menu' appeared three centuries ago, the modern menu listing a choice of dishes didn't really come into play until the early 19th century. In fine restaurants, these menus were grandiose affairs with hundreds of dishes listed and barely recognisable as what we use today.

The prime raison d'être of the menu is, of course, to inform the diner what there is to eat and how much it will cost. There are as many thoughts on how a good menu should be written as there are chefs. The

BEROWRA
WATERS INN

23rd – 25th July 2010

Our menu is designed as a series of 'degustation' or tasting dishes. Please select the number
of dishes you would like to enjoy, or if you would prefer the chef would be delighted to select
the dishes for you. Our dishes are listed so you may enjoy a progression
down the menu, with or without... the wines matched by the glass by our sommelier...

o

Chilled Vichyssoise, Oscietra & Salmon Caviars, Beignets Of Hawkesbury Oysters
Hewitson 'Gun Metal' Riesling 2009, Eden Valley, South Australia

White Asparagus, Green Asparagus, Slow Poached Organic Egg Yolk.
Fresh Black Winter Truffle From Manjimup
Kinkenwood (Biodynamic) Chardonnay 2008, Hunter Valley, New South Wales

Grilled Sea Scallops, Cauliflower, Pickled Salsify, Salted Walnuts, Green Apple
Scarborough 'Green Label' Semillon 2009, Hunter Valley, New South Wales

Buffalo Mozzarella, Espelette Pepper, Potato Gnocchi, Wild Mushrooms, Sage Butter
Tim Smith Viognier 2009, Adelaide Hills, South Australia

Australian Marron, Fermented Garlic, Sweet Green Peas, Alsace Bacon
Joseph Drouhin Chablis 2008, Burgundy, France

[...] Celeriac, Croustillant Of Peppered Oxtail
[...] Blanc / Semillon 2009, Margaret River, Western Australia

[...] Duck, Foie Gras, Oriental Consommé
[...] ng, Marlborough, New Zealand

[...] Spinach, Roast Shallot Jus
[...] y, Victoria

[...] eetbread,
[...] NSW/SA

verbiage used by some chefs makes *War and Peace* look like a novelette; the spareness of prose of others leaves the guests pondering what exactly they have ordered. 'Fillet of Tasmanian salmon blended with organic eggs and cream from Old McDonald's farm before being poached in an aromatic court bouillon and served on baby vegetables handpicked from Mr McGregor's garden at 2.30 this morning' may be true, but it is too much information if you are going to eat the dish in the restaurant and not enough if you want to cook it at home.

I started writing menus in the early 1980s when it was the fashion to describe the main ingredients and their exact preparation in detail, and also pinpoint the geographic location of the hill where the lamb lived its short life or identify the fisherman who 'hand-dived' the scallop. Most restaurants have abandoned this method of describing dishes and menus have been abbreviated to more essential information.

However, that information isn't always true, which leads me to one of my pet peeves … menu honesty. This problem ranges from lying about the provenance of ingredients to describing the preparation wrongly. The latter is annoying but the first is misleading and dishonest. If it is not organic then don't say it is, if it isn't 'wagyu' beef then claiming it is will only disappoint. If it is 'silver dory' rather than 'john dory', then say so! Another annoying practice is to use subjective words on a menu. Words such as 'delicious', 'tasty', 'tender', and so on, are pointless because they are assessing the dish qualitatively— and that surely is up to the diner, not the chef. And

CANAPÉ OF EGGS AND CHIPS'

when it comes to the accuracy of spelling on the menu … well, don't get me started!

A good menu will be well balanced and convey the chef's respect for the seasons. It will inform the diner of the cooking style, the seasonings and provenance of the ingredients. It will highlight any items that a guest may take exception to, such as garlic and chilli. It will tantalise the taste buds without overpromising, create table conversation, start a dialogue between the diner and the waiter. Browsing a menu with an aperitif in hand is, or should be, one of life's great pleasures … no wonder the great 19th-century chef Auguste Escoffier wrote that 'a good menu is difficult to compose'.

A menu can also tell experienced diners a lot about an establishment before they enter the front doors. If it is excessively large and the restaurant has few staff, chances are the freezer will play a large role or the dishes are just not getting the attention they deserve. But if the menu is small and the kitchen staffed with a large battery of chefs, you are in for at best a special dining experience and at worst a meal stuffed and sauced to within an inch of its life (along with a chef who will drive you crazy with little touches). Pricing, of course, indicates the restaurant's pretensions. Do not be misled though: many people confuse value for money with the cost of dining. 'Grilled Fillet of Wagyu Beef with Truffles' in a casual restaurant at $39 is likely to be a low-grade wagyu, if it is indeed wagyu, and you will need a magnifying glass to find the truffles. A $150 per head degustation in a top restaurant may be excellent value in comparison because you will get six or more courses of high-quality ingredients.

Sugar-cured Salmon, Spiced Avocado, Crisp Tortilla

8 coriander seeds

30g (1oz) sea salt

30g (1oz) sugar

20g (^{2}/$_3$oz) dill sprigs, roughly chopped

1 lime, zested, juice reserved

zest of 1 lemon

400g (14oz) centre-cut salmon fillet, skin on,
    pin-boned

30ml (1fl oz) lemon-infused extra virgin olive oil

SPICED AVOCADO

1 ripe Hass avocado

2tsp shallot, finely chopped

^{1}/$_2$tsp red chilli, finely diced

20ml (^{2}/$_3$fl oz) chicken stock, chilled

juice of 1 lime (above)

sea salt

TO COMPLETE

2 large soft flour tortillas

grapeseed oil for frying

sea salt

30g (1oz) salmon roe

micro coriander leaves

◆ This canapé—a classic combination of salmon and avocado served on a crisp tortilla—can easily be turned into an entrée. Assemble it at the last moment so you have a warm, crisp tortilla counterbalancing the cool avocado and sugar-cured salmon. The best wine to accompany this would be a glass of champagne or a crisp riesling.

FOR THE SUGAR-CURED SALMON: Place the coriander seeds, sea salt and sugar in a mortar and lightly crush with a pestle. Add the dill, lime and lemon zests and spread evenly over the flesh side of the salmon.

Wrap the salmon in clingfilm or aluminium foil and place on a plate with a light weight on top. Leave the weighted salmon in the fridge for 4 hours, then wash the fish under cold running water and dry well with a clean cloth.

Using a sharp knife, remove the salmon fillet from the skin. Rub the salmon with a little lemon-infused extra virgin olive oil and keep tightly wrapped in the fridge until needed.

FOR THE SPICED AVOCADO: Cut the avocado in half, discard the stone and scoop out the flesh. Place the avocado flesh in a blender along with the shallots, chilli and chicken stock. Blend to a puree and correct the seasoning with the lime juice and some sea salt.

TO COMPLETE: Cut the tortillas into rectangles and crisp-fry in some grapeseed oil. Remove and season lightly with sea salt. Spoon some avocado puree on top of the warm tortilla and then place a slice of the sugar-cured salmon on the avocado. Garnish with salmon roe and some micro coriander leaves.

MAKES 18 CANAPÉS

Buffalo Mozzarella, Eggplant Caviar, Tomato Chilli Coulis

EGGPLANT CAVIAR

1 medium eggplant (aubergine)

1 clove garlic, finely chopped

3 shallots, finely chopped

$^1/_2$tsp red chilli, finely chopped

1tsp orange zest, finely chopped

2 anchovies, washed and chopped

8 green peppercorns

1tsp coriander, chopped

1tsp flatleaf parsley, finely chopped

lemon juice

extra virgin olive oil

TO SERVE

2 large soft flour tortillas

grapeseed oil for frying

sea salt

4 balls fresh buffalo milk mozzarella

extra virgin olive oil

50ml ($1^3/_4$fl oz) tomato chilli coulis (see recipe, page 263)

18 small basil leaves

◆ I love eggplant 'caviar'. In this canapé the warm, soft eggplant is combined with chilled fresh mozzarella and offset by the crisp tortilla and a dash of heat from the tomato chilli coulis. Eat it with a glass of champagne spiked with a dash of vodka or a gewürztraminer.

FOR THE EGGPLANT CAVIAR: Preheat the oven to 150°C (300°F). Cut the eggplant in half and rub the cut sides with the extra virgin olive oil. Wrap each half in aluminium foil, place on a tray and bake in the oven until the eggplant is soft.

Scoop out the pulp and discard the skins. Leave the eggplant pulp in a colander to drain for an hour.

Sweat the garlic, shallots, chilli and orange zest in a little olive oil until soft but not coloured. Add the anchovies, peppercorns and the eggplant pulp and slowly cook until the pulp dries out. Remove from the stove and season with the chopped herbs, lemon juice and sea salt.

TO SERVE: Cut the tortillas into 3cm (1¼in) rounds and crisp-fry in some grapeseed oil. Remove and season lightly with sea salt; keep warm. Cut the mozzarella into 5mm (¼in) slices and then the slices into 2.5cm (1in) rounds. Season with sea salt and drizzle with extra virgin olive oil. Spoon the warm eggplant caviar on each tortilla and top with a slice of mozzarella and then with some tomato chilli coulis. Garnish with a sweet basil leaf and serve.

MAKES 18 CANAPÉS

Canapé of 'Eggs and Chips'

2 large potatoes, preferably rustic
   burbank
500ml (17^{1}/$_{2}$fl oz) chicken stock
grapeseed oil for frying

120g (4oz) oscietra caviar or salmon roe
50ml sour cream
micro dill leaves

◆   This is a fun play on the classic English dish of 'egg and chips'. Potatoes are a perfect vehicle for caviar and, matched with a glass of champagne or a chilled vodka, they make a stylish way to prelude a meal.

FOR THE CHIPS: Preheat the oven to 60°C (140°F). Peel the potatoes and cut into large chips approximately 1 x 1 x 5cm (½ x ½ x 2in). Poach the chips in the chicken stock until they are just cooked. Drain and place on a tray in the oven for an hour to dry them.

In a deep-fryer, heat the grapeseed oil to 120°C (250°F) and fry the chips until they start to colour. Remove from the fryer and drain on absorbent paper. Chill until ready to use them.

TO COMPLETE: Reheat the oil to 180°C (350°F) and fry the chips until golden brown. Remove and shake off excess oil. Spread each chip with caviar or salmon roe and top with sour cream and the dill leaves. Serve warm.

MAKES 4 SERVINGS

Tartare of Yellowfin Tuna, Avocado, Asian Flavours

POTATO CRISPS

2 large potatoes, starchy variety

2 Tbsp clarified butter, melted

sea salt

wasabi paste to taste

TUNA TARTARE

1 avocado

1 lemon

sea salt

freshly ground white pepper

400g (14oz) tuna, sashimi quality

wasabi paste to taste

1 Tbsp mayonnaise (see recipe, page 263)

2 limes

2 shallots, finely diced

1 Tbsp pickled ginger, finely diced

1 red chilli, finely diced

1 Tbsp chives, finely snipped

2 Tbsp Japanese pure sesame oil

TO SERVE

3 tsp wasabi-flavoured flying fish roe

2 lime leaves, julienned

◆ Tuna is one of those fish that is best eaten raw. Here we complement it with lovely Asian flavours for a change.

FOR THE POTATO CRISPS: Preheat the oven to 200°C (400°F). Trim the potatoes into oval shapes and then thinly slice on a mandolin to 2mm ($^1/_8$in) thickness. Toss together in a bowl with the melted clarified butter and season with sea salt.

Cover a baking sheet with silicone or baking paper. Lay half the potato slices on the sheet and then smear each of them with wasabi paste. Place the other potato slices evenly on top of the wasabi-smeared potatoes and place a sheet of silicone paper on top. Bake the potatoes in the heated oven until crisp and golden brown.

FOR THE TUNA TARTARE: Finely dice the avocado and season with a little lemon juice, sea salt and ground white pepper.

Cut the tuna into 5mm (¼in) dice and place in a bowl. Mix a little wasabi paste with the mayonnaise to taste and then lightly bind the tuna with the mayonnaise. Season with a little lime juice, shallots, the pickled ginger, chilli, chives and sesame oil.

TO COMPLETE: Spoon some of the tuna tartare on each potato crisp and top with a little flying fish roe and the julienned lime leaves.

MAKES 24 CANAPÉS

Our Duck Prosciutto, Prawn and Celeriac Remoulade, Toasted Brazil Nuts

DUCK PROSCIUTTO

15g (¹/₂oz) sea salt, crushed

1 tsp caster sugar

6 coriander seeds, crushed

6 white peppercorns, crushed

2 sprigs lemon thyme

zest of 1 orange

300g (10oz) duck breast

20g (²/₃oz) ground white pepper

PRAWN & CELERIAC REMOULADE

60g (2oz) celeriac, julienned

30ml (1fl oz) sauce remoulade (see recipe, page 261)

squeeze of lemon juice to taste

6 cooked king prawns, shelled and deveined

TO SERVE

6 brazil nuts

30g (1oz) butter

pinch of smoked sea salt

1 tsp chopped chives

◆ Duck prosciutto is easy to make and is a lovely way to use duck. Here it is combined with crisp fresh prawns, subtle celeriac and toasted brazil nuts. Of course, the prawn and celeriac remoulade makes a lovely dish all on its own. You need to start this recipe at least seven days before you plan to eat it. The best wine option would be a pinot grigio.

FOR THE DUCK PROSCIUTTO: Combine the sea salt and sugar with coriander seeds, white peppercorns, lemon thyme and orange zest. Place in a bowl with the duck breast and massage the mixture into the flesh. Wrap the duck and the mixture in aluminium foil and refrigerate for 24 hours to cure.

Wash the duck breast off under cold running water and dry it well. Dust with the ground white pepper to stop any bacteria growing on the duck and wrap it in a muslin cloth. Hang in a temperature-controlled area or cool room (8–15°C/46.4–59°F) for a minimum of seven days. When ready, remove the duck from the muslin and rub with olive oil. Vacuum pack until needed or use within the week.

FOR THE PRAWN AND CELERIAC REMOULADE: Toss the julienned celeriac with the sauce remoulade and a squeeze of lemon juice. Season to taste with sea salt. Slice the prawns and toss through the celeriac salad.

TO SERVE: Thinly slice the duck prosciutto. Arrange the celeriac salad in Chinese spoons and top with a slice of duck prosciutto. Slice the brazil nuts and sauté in the butter until golden. Garnish each spoon with a slice of brazil nut, a pinch of smoked sea salt and chopped chives.

MAKES 18 CANAPÉS

2

FIRST COURSE

YELLOWFIN TUNA PEPPER STEAK

The history of the Inn—the early years

One of things that first attracted me to Berowra Waters Inn is that it has possibly the longest and most fascinating history of any eating establishment in Australia.

The Aboriginal civilisation is one of the oldest in the world and at Berowra Waters the evidence is everywhere. The Aboriginal name for Berowra was 'Besoora', which means 'windy place' or 'meeting of the winds'.

During the reconstruction work carried out on the building by Tony and Gay Bilson in the 1970s, shells from an Aboriginal midden were uncovered in the cellar and Tony had them carbon dated—with somewhat startling results. The oldest piece dated from around ten thousand years ago. Theoretically,

that means the site is possibly one of the oldest 'restaurants' in the world.

Closer to our times, the public ferry crossing the Hawkesbury River at Berowra, an hour north of Sydney, was completed in 1902. It was never intended for vehicles, although at a struggle it could later manage four cars, which were hand-winched on and off until 1931, when it was fitted with a 5-horsepower motor. Back then, people would leave their horses on the eastern edge of the river, along what has become Kirkpatrick Way, much as residents and visitors to the restaurant do with their cars now. Telephones were introduced in 1927, but the service hasn't been improved much—the same exchange is still in place and it just manages to cope with the

demands of the increased population and with broadband internet.

Riverview House, an old woolwash building that was converted to a restaurant and was the southern-most property at Berowra Waters, was the first true restaurant in the area. Run by Millie and Dan Cullen, it was 'highly recommended' by the media of the time and charged two shillings and sixpence for a 'very filling' meal of local fish and oysters.

Berowra Waters was an extremely popular tourist destination and also the home of many well-known actors during the 1920s and '30s. In the hot months, up to three thousand people would catch the train from the city and walk down to the river each weekend.

Berowra Waters Inn was originally the Pacific Private Guest House, operated by Bobby and Ted Withers from 1926 to 1946. Ted camped in Deep Bay for ten years while he built it. The stone wall at the front of the restaurant is from his original building and was constructed by Ted after his architect suggested that the large rock on the site had to be removed. A Swiss couple purchased the building in the early 1950s and for the first time European cordon bleu food was served to the growing numbers of holidaymakers on the river. Sadly, after more than 20 years, the chef started losing her sight and they sold the property in 1970.

After several changes of ownership, the Bilsons bought the property in 1976. That's another story.

About the importance of *mise en place*

Mise en place literally means 'to put in place', but in a culinary sense it is so much more than that—it is almost a state of mind as well as a physical process. In the professional kitchen, it is essential to have a good *mise en place*, otherwise you are going to be in trouble very quickly. In its simplest terms, *mise en place* means to prepare, pre-measure and even pre-cook certain items. More generally, it also means that you are organised—that you have everything ready needed to complete each dish. It is about a flowing, time-saving cooking and serving process.

The only way a professional kitchen can operate smoothly and turn out the amount of meals in the timeframe required is to have a good *mise en place*.

This also applies to home cooks. How many times have you jumped into a recipe only to discover step four requires a vital ingredient that should have been prepared earlier? Suddenly everything come to a standstill while you backtrack, resulting in frustration, stress and wasted time.

How far should *mise en place* go? At the far end of the scale, the meal can be fully prepared and sealed in 'sous-vide' vacuum bags and just need reheating, or it might mean just assembling the ingredients and peeling or chopping them to the required size.

I was one of the first chefs to be invited to be a member of Singapore Airlines' World Gourmet Culinary Panel. Working with airline food was totally new to me and completely different to the high-class dining I was accustomed to. In restaurants we do as

much as possible at the last minute; with airline food you do as little as you can at the last minute.

The more expensive the restaurant, usually the larger the kitchen brigade. The larger the kitchen brigade, the more that can be done *à la minute*, at the last minute, which means that the *mise en place* time can be taken up with ever more complex preparations.

Whether at home or in the professional kitchen, having a correct *mise en place* means that you are already 80 per cent of the way to producing a quality dish.

Thoughts on remote restaurants

There is a general rule that restaurants at the top of tall buildings and restaurants that move are not good to eat in. There are exceptions to every rule, of course, and such restaurants as my Forty One in Sydney and Jules Verne in the Eiffel Tower in Paris prove that fine food and high buildings can go together. I would like to propose a new rule: that the more remote a restaurant is, the better it is—the logic being that if you are going to put a restaurant in an out-of-the-way location, then you better make sure it is worth the trip.

For the purpose of my theory, I must define 'remote' as being in a location that is difficult to get to and thus requires additional effort on the part of the diners. Michel Bras's wonderful restaurant on top of

a windswept hill in Laguiole in the French Pyrenees is one of several with three Michelin stars in remote locations. But at least these restaurants have roads that come up to the door. Truly remote restaurants require alternative transport like one on a northern Italian lake— it is housed in a natural grotto, which can only be accessed by boat, and it serves the most wonderful seafood. Another I know is on the highest hiking track in Europe and can only be got to by foot in summer and on skis in winter—to sit there and enjoy a bottle of wine and long lunch is to know serenity. What these restaurants and others like them, including our beloved piece of heaven on earth here at Berowra, have in common is a desire to make a magical spot even better by providing the best in food and wine that they can, despite the logistics.

For logistics are what it is all about. Everything from the cooking fuel to the toilet paper, from the toothpicks to the caviar, must be brought in and then any refuse and by-products taken out—and whether by boat, by ski-mobile or by donkey, it takes good organisation and a lot of hard manual labour.

Roasted Lobster-stuffed Chicken Wings, Cauliflower, Basil

~~~

6 large chicken wings

250ml (9fl oz) poultry brine (see
    recipe, page xxx)

clarified butter for cooking

sea salt

250ml (9fl oz) beurre veloute (see
    recipe, page xxx)

juice of 1 lemon

LOBSTER FARCE

3 x 600g (20oz) live lobsters

1tsp dried shiitake mushroom

1tsp Japanese pickled ginger

90ml (3fl oz) cream

CAULIFLOWER PUREE

250g (9oz) cauliflower

250ml (9fl oz) chicken stock

125ml (4^1/$_2$fl oz) cream

25g butter

TO SERVE

2tsp tomato dice (see recipe, page xx)

baby basil leaves

60ml (2fl oz) basil oil (see recipe, page xx)

◆   I have always loved the unctuousness of chicken wings. As children, we used to fight over the wings of the freshly roasted chicken. I enjoy pairing the simple with the luxurious—here, raising the roast chicken wing to fine dining heights by adding lobster. You could easily do the same dish with prawns. The cauliflower puree adds a nice counterbalance to the salty wings and the basil oil brings it all together in harmony. We would normally serve a New Zealand sauvignon blanc or maybe a French sancerre with this dish.

PREPARING THE CHICKEN WINGS: Remove the drumette (the wing bone attached to the breast bone) from the chicken wings and reserve for another dish. Leaving the wing tip still on, lay the wing on a chopping board and, using the tip of a small knife, carefully cut around the membranes holding the two small bones in place. Once you have cut these membranes, use your fingers to 'peel' the chicken skin and meat back until you have exposed a centimetre (about ½ inch) of the two bones. Take the top of the two bones in one hand and the rest of the wing in the other and strip the meat back in a sharp movement, ending with a twist of the wrist to snap the bones free. This may take a little practice but once you have the technique you will be able to debone wings in a flash.

Once you have deboned all the wings, soak them in poultry brine for 1 hour while you make the lobster farce.

PREPARING THE LOBSTER: Using a towel or rubber gloves to hold the lobster, grasp its tail and twist the body in the opposite direction to its head to remove the tail. Place the lobster tail on a board and cut down between the two segments of the shell at the end of the tail; the medallion you end up with will be oddly shaped so remove the meat from the shell. Next, cut two more medallions using the same method: you should end up with two nice even medallions in their shell. With the remaining piece of the tail, split lengthways down through the centre of the shell and remove the meat; add it to the meat from the first medallion. Repeat the process with the other two lobster tails. At the end you should have six neat medallions, a pile of lobster meat and some shells.

Split the head carcasses and remove the tomalley (the paste or 'mustard'), roe, lungs and sac behind the head. Rinse well and reserve, or freeze, to make a lobster bisque, consommé or sauce later.

FOR THE LOBSTER FARCE: Place the lobster meat, shiitake mushrooms and pickled ginger in a food processor and blitz quickly. Season lightly with a pinch of sea salt and blitz again for 30 seconds. Add the cream and give a final blitz to amalgamate. Check the seasoning by poaching a little bit of the farce in some boiling water. Add a little more sea salt if needed.

FOR THE CAULIFLOWER PUREE: Bring the chicken stock to the boil and reduce by half. Add the cream and bring back to the boil. Cut the cauliflower into small, evenly sized florets, add to the boiling liquid and cook for a few minutes until tender. Remove the pan from the heat and strain off the liquid, reserving it. Place the hot cauliflower in a blender and add a little of the cooking liquor. Blend until you have a smooth puree. Put the puree in a clean saucepan over low heat and whisk in the cold butter. Check the seasoning and correct with sea salt if needed.

STUFFING THE CHICKEN WINGS: Remove the chicken wings from the brine, drain on paper towels and dry well. Using a disposable piping bag, pipe some farce into the open end of each chicken wing— do not overfill as the farce will expand as it cooks. Secure the open end of the wing with a toothpick.

COOKING THE CHICKEN AND LOBSTER: Preheat the oven to 200°C (400°F). When they are all stuffed, add the wings, top side down, to a hot ovenproof frying pan with a little clarified butter. Lightly brown the wings in the butter and then place the frying pan in the hot oven and roast the wings until golden brown, about 5–8 minutes. Remove the pan from the oven and rest for a couple of minutes.

Meanwhile, heat the beurre veloute. Place the lobster medallions in a pan and season with sea salt. Pour over the warm beurre veloute and cook over a low heat for 5 minutes. Remove the lobster from the beurre veloute and sprinkle with lemon juice.

TO SERVE: Slice the wing tip off the chicken wing and then slice the wing into two or three slices, depending on its size. Place a small spoonful of cauliflower puree on each plate. Arrange one lobster medallion and the sliced chicken wing on the puree, garnish with the diced tomato and baby basil leaves. Drizzle with the basil oil just before serving.

MAKES 6 SERVINGS

Roasted Lobster-stuffed Chicken Wings, Cauliflower, Basil

Seared Kangaroo Carpaccio, Warm Kipfler Potato, Fresh Winter Truffle

CARPACCIO

2 kangaroo loin fillets

sea salt

freshly ground black pepper

40ml (1^1/$_2$fl oz) aged balsamic vinegar

40ml (1^1/$_2$fl oz) extra virgin olive oil

KIPFLER POTATOES

150g (5oz) kipfler potatoes, washed, skins on

25g (^{3}/$_4$oz) shallot confit (see recipe,
    page 264)

100ml (3^1/$_2$fl oz) truffle vinaigrette (see recipe,
    page 262)

TO SERVE

10g (^{1}/$_3$oz) fresh black winter truffle

10g (^{1}/$_3$oz) chives, finely sliced

20g (^{2}/$_3$oz) chervil sprigs

◆ Potatoes and truffles are a great combination and here I have paired them with a seared carpaccio of kangaroo. Kangaroo is a lovely, gamey meat that in my opinion is best served raw or very rare because it has little fat and can easily become dry when cooked. A gamay or pinot noir would best suit this dish.

FOR THE CARPACCIO: Season the kangaroo fillets well. Heat a grill plate or cast iron pan and quickly sear the meat, about 30 seconds on each side. Remove from the pan and place on a sheet of clingfilm. Roll it up tightly, forming a cylinder, and leave to cool.

FOR THE KIPFLER POTATOES: Boil the kipfler potatoes in salted water until they are easily pierced with a knife, about 15–20 minutes. Drain and while still warm peel the skins off and discard. Slice the potatoes and toss with the shallot confit and truffle vinaigrette. Season with sea salt. Keep at room temperature until ready to serve.

TO SERVE: Slice the kangaroo finely and place in a bowl. Season with sea salt and dress with the aged balsamic vinegar and extra virgin olive oil. Leave for a couple of minutes and then drain. Cover the base of four plates with a mosaic of kangaroo slices. Neatly dress a pile of the truffled potato salad in the middle of each plate of kangaroo. Place generous slices of the fresh truffle on each and sprinkle with chopped chives and chervil sprigs.

MAKES 4 SERVINGS

Galantine of Quail, Foie Gras, Lillet Jelly, Toasted Brioche

QUAIL GALANTINE

4 quails, boned

80g (2¹/₂oz) foie gras (goose liver), cooked

6 large spinach leaves, blanched

100g (3¹/₂oz) crepinette (pig's caul—order
   from your butcher)

pinch of smoked sea salt

LILLET JELLY

200ml (7fl oz) Lillet apertif wine

30g (1oz) sugar

2 sheets gelatine, titanium-strength

TO SERVE

4 slices brioche, toasted

◆ We cannot get fresh foie gras in Australia so this is a way to serve the pre-cooked foie gras from France. Combining the Chinese technique of 'white-cut chicken', we are able to serve a delicate silky quail with the melting creaminess of foie gras through the centre. The best wine to accompany this would be a glass of a favourite French aperitif wine, Lillet, or a sauternes.

FOR THE QUAIL GALANTINE: Remove any small bones from two of the quails and lay them out on the bench, skin side down, to form a square. Cut the breasts from the remaining two quails and remove the skin. Also remove the skin from the boned quail legs. Using the cut breasts and leg meat, fill in any 'holes' in the laid-out square—you should end up with a neat square of quail meat with the skin underneath.

Wrap the foie gras in the blanched spinach leaves. Place the spinach-wrapped foie gras on the quail 'square' and then roll up the quail to form a cylinder. Wrap the cylinder in crepinette and then tightly in clingfilm. Wrap this in foil and place in a saucepan of warm water, held at 55°C (131°F), and gently cook for 40 minutes. Remove from the water and plunge into an ice bath to chill quickly.

FOR THE LILLET JELLY: Heat the Lillet with the sugar. When warm, dissolve the gelatine leaves in the Lillet and pour into a tray to set. When set, 'rough up' the jelly with a fork.

TO SERVE: Slice the quail galantine into four equal portions. Place on plates and brush the top of the galantine with a little olive oil, add a spoon of the Lillet jelly and serve with the warm toasted brioche.

MAKES 4 SERVINGS

Chilled Vichyssoise, Oscietra Caviar, Beignets of Hawkesbury Oysters

VICHYSSOISE

30g (1oz) butter

350g (12oz) leeks, finely sliced

150g (5oz) white onions, finely sliced

175g (6oz) potatoes, peeled and evenly diced

25ml ($^3/_4$fl oz) Chinese oyster sauce (optional)

700ml (24$^1/_2$fl oz) white chicken stock, warm

150ml (5oz) cream

4 sheets gelatine, titanium-strength

2 gas chargers for cream siphon

OYSTER BEIGNETS

1 leek, finely sliced

20g ($^2/_3$oz) butter

50ml (1$^3/_4$fl oz) dry white wine

100ml (3$^1/_2$fl oz) cream

8 Hawkesbury oysters

rice flour for dusting

1 recipe beignet batter (see recipes, page 259)

TO COMPLETE

40g (1$^1/_2$oz) oscietra caviar

40g (1$^1/_2$oz) salmon roe

20g ($^2/_3$oz) mini croutons (see recipes, page 265)

2tsp chives, finely sliced

◆ This is the only dish that has been on the Berowra menu continually since we opened. It is a new take on the classic chilled soup of vichyssoise and, when paired with caviar and the crisp warm beignets of local oysters, it raises this classic dish to new levels. The vichyssoise recipe makes approximately 1 litre (35fl oz)—you'll need about half that for this dish. It is best suited to a glass of champagne or a crisp riesling.

FOR THE VICHYSSOISE: Melt the butter in a stainless steel saucepan over moderate heat and add the leeks and onions. Cover and 'sweat' without colouring until the vegetables are tender, about 8–10 minutes. Add the diced potatoes and the oyster sauce (if using) and stir well. Pour in the warm chicken stock and bring to the boil. Simmer, covered, for about 15 minutes, until the potatoes are cooked through and starting to break down. Add the cream, bring back to the boil for a couple of minutes. Remove from the stove and allow to cool for 15 minutes.

Taste for seasoning and adjust with sea salt if necessary. Add the gelatine leaves and stir well. Using a high-speed blender, blend the vichyssoise and then chill in the refrigerator. When the soup has fully chilled and set in the fridge, spoon the mixture into a cream whipper canister and charge up with two gas cartridges. Shake well and keep chilled until needed.

FOR THE OYSTER BEIGNETS: Sweat the sliced leeks in the butter, covered, until they are tender but not coloured, about 8–10 minutes. Remove the lid and add the white wine, reduce until the wine has

CONTINUES ON PAGE 52

evaporated and then add the cream and season with sea salt. Cover and cook gently until the leeks are soft and the cream has reduced.

Open the oysters. Keep the bottom halve of each shell and wash carefully to remove any chips. Warm the shells in the oven.

TO COMPLETE: Reheat the leeks and spoon some into each oyster shell and keep warm. Using a demitasse cup, foam some of the vichyssoise into the cup to half-fill it. Spoon in some oscietra caviar and salmon roe, fill the cups with more vichyssoise foam and sprinkle the top of each with mini croutons and chopped chives.

Toss the oysters in a little rice flour and shake off the excess. Dip them in batter and quickly fry them in 250°C (482°F) oil. Drain and then place them in each half-shell over the creamed leeks. Arrange the oyster shells on a bed of rock salt next to the demitasse of vichyssoise.

MAKES 4 SERVINGS

Tartare of Beef Fillet, Crisp Onion Rings, Truffle Jelly, Mushroom Salad

TARTARE OF BEEF FILLET

400g (14oz) beef fillet, coarsely minced

2 small cornichons, finely diced

1tsp baby capers, washed and chopped

2tsp shallots, finely chopped

1 large egg yolk

dash of Tabasco sauce

$^1/_4$tsp mustard

2tsp tomato ketchup

dash of Worcestershire sauce

1tsp chopped chives

$^1/_4$tsp chopped red chilli

sea salt

CRISP ONION RINGS

1 spanish onion, sliced into rings

flour for dusting

100ml ($3^1/_2$fl oz) beignet batter (see recipe, page 259)

MUSHROOM SALAD

30g (1oz) butter

2 cloves garlic

250g (9oz) mixed mushrooms

sea salt

200ml (7fl oz) à la greque mixture (see recipe, page xxx)

1tsp tarragon, finely chopped

1tsp chives, finely chopped

TO COMPLETE

yolks of 4 quail eggs

60ml (2fl oz) truffle jelly (see recipe, page 262)

8 sprigs chervil

20g ($^2/_3$oz) fresh truffles, sliced

◆ Steak tartare is my favourite way to eat beef. Here I match the cold tartare with a warm mushroom salad, which really highlights the flavours of each. The more varieties of mushrooms you use the better— I suggest shiitakes, shemiji, chanterelles and swiss browns. Gamay or pinot noir set this off perfectly.

FOR THE TARTARE OF BEEF FILLET: Place the minced beef in a cold bowl, add all the other ingredients and mix well. Adjust the seasoning with sea salt and Tabasco and/or Worcestershire sauce if needed.

FOR THE CRISP ONION RINGS: Separate the onion rings. Season, toss in flour. and dredge in batter. Deep-fry in grapeseed oil at 180°C (350°F) until golden. Drain on absorbent paper. Sprinkle with sea salt.

FOR THE MUSHROOM SALAD: Melt the butter in a pan and add the garlic. When it starts to brown, add the mushrooms and gently sauté until golden. Taste and correct the seasoning. Add the à la greque mix and bring to the boil. Remove from the heat and pour into a jar. When needed, drain the mushrooms, sauté in a little butter and toss with chopped tarragon and chives.

TO COMPLETE: With a ring mould, make a neat 'pattie' of the tartare on four plates. Smooth the top. In the middle of each make a small indentation and insert a quail egg yolk. Arrange the warm mushroom salad, truffle jelly and onion rings around the tartare. Garnish with chervil and truffle slices.

MAKES 4 SERVINGS

CEAN COURSE

On food as art

If restaurant publicists and chefs are to be believed, there are an awful lot of artists out there baking bread, rolling pasta, making sauces and tossing salads!

The argument over whether food and cooking is art has been waged for many years now by people who have nothing better to do. Is a chef an artist or craftsperson? Strangely enough, such a seemingly irrelevant question will often engender the hottest debate among a group of food professionals. It would seem to me that it is not a black-and-white question but, like most things in life, it is all shades of grey.

First and foremost is the definition of 'artist'. If you consider that a true artist must be free to have an original artistic inspiration, then the very nature of the job of a chef, who must reproduce his work consistently night after night, precludes the chef from being an artist and firmly places him in the category of artisan.

However, if the term 'artist' is broadened to mean the creation of something unique that gives sensory pleasure then, yes, a chef may be an artist … of course, using that criterion it might be argued that Enzo Ferrari or indeed your local talented plumber is also an artist. If you are arguing about the aesthetics of food—beautifully arranged, delicious food, full of wonderful tastes and textures, which is perfectly prepared—then it certainly could be considered art. But who is the artist: the chef who created it or the chef who cooked it?

Of course, anyone involved in the 'real art world' would decry this definition as simplistic and say that a chef could not be an artist because of her inbuilt desire—indeed, need—to please her guests. A real artist wishes to express her own vision, whether it is pleasing or not. A chef who did not offer diners something good to eat would not be a chef for long, but an artist who produces an ugly painting or installation is still an artist.

But is it fair that the senses of taste and smell are not afforded 'an artist' to cater to them? Certainly, the composition of a new dish is akin to that of a piece of music or a painting: it requires the same mastery of the subject, complex skills and inspiration. The disciplines

required for painting and sculpture are closely mirrored in the professional kitchen. The level of performance expected from a great restaurant is no different from that of a great ballet company or an orchestra.

The recent development of high-tech cooking equipment, and the molecular gastronomy this had led to, certainly highlights the scientific nature of cooking. In the past, cooks learned various techniques to achieve particular results without really questioning why they were doing what they were doing. When Harold McGee published his book *On Food and Cooking* in 1984, I am sure he didn't realise what an impact it would make on modern cooking techniques. This book by a young American professor from Yale explores the scientific reasons behind the methods that cooks routinely used, methods such as searing meat or whipping egg whites. Mr McGee spent 700 pages explaining the science of the kitchen, all in plain, simple language. What he achieved was to open the eyes of a new generation of chefs who began questioning the culinary principles they had been taught. Cooking is a series of chemical reactions and scientific principles, after all. It is only

ICED CHOCOLATE BON BONS

after applying these scientific methods and processes that we enter what can be considered the artistic part of cooking—that is, arranging the food to make it look attractive.

There are no definitive answers to these questions. Even if we believe a chef can be considered an artist, certainly not every snotty-nosed kid who dons some chef's whites can be considered one. So who decides? Luckily, this is all irrelevant to the enjoyment of food and restaurants. Let the philosophical debate rage among those who care—all I know is that, artist or artisan, producing great food is bloody hard work.

Thoughts about shellfish

Australia is abundant in exoskeleton-bearing aquatic invertebrates that can be used as food—what we in the culinary world call shellfish. The term 'shellfish' covers a wide spectrum of species, including but not limited to the many varieties of oyster, crab, mussels, winkles, scallops, prawns, lobsters, yabbies, marrons and even sea urchins. Although most kinds of shellfish are harvested from saltwater environments, my favourite is the freshwater yabby. It is a sweet-tasting little clawed shellfish similar to the European *ecrevises pattes rouge* but slightly larger. These native shellfish are widely farmed and never off the menu.

Here at Berowra Waters it is a particular pleasure to pull fresh mud crabs of over 2 kilograms (4lb 6oz)

out of our restaurant's crab pots, especially when the crabs are plentiful between January and April. As we are on the upper reaches of the Hawkesbury, the river is still saltwater turning to brackish and it is very tidal.

We get fantastic oysters from a grower about 15 minutes upstream. These juicy, plump oysters are taken from the water at Broken Bay in the morning and delivered by boat to the restaurant for lunch. Any we don't open are returned to the water to grow a bit more for next week. Now, that is fresh.

The Hawkesbury River is also famous for its squid and school prawns, both of which feature regularly on our changing weekly menu. The local squid is silky and a delight to work with—it is so good it seems a shame to cook it.

With such a large coastline of mainly pristine waters and Australia's largest seafood markets in Sydney, we get plenty of choice to supplement our local product: the larger prawns from Yamba, wonderful sea scallops from Queensland, pacific oysters from Tasmania, yabbies from Kangaroo Island in South Australia and wonderful mediaeval-looking marron from Western Australia. My biggest challenge when constructing the menu is deciding which to leave out. The only member of the genre I rarely use is the Australian lobster. The local variety is a spiny lobster, so doesn't have claws and is nice enough, but the supply is unsteady and the prices ridiculous because most of them end up in the Asian markets. But, with the abundance of other local shellfish, we don't really miss them.

Steamed Kangaroo Island Yabbies, Risotto alla Milanese

RISOTTO ALLA MILANESE

2Tbsp extra virgin olive oil

2Tbsp butter

4 shallots, finely chopped

200g (7oz) vialoni nano or arborio rice

$^1/_2$tsp saffron powder

600ml (20fl oz) chicken stock

50g (1$^3/_4$oz) fontina cheese, grated

75g (2$^1/_2$oz) bone marrow, finely chopped
   (optional)

THE YABBIES

16 yabbies, each at least 100g (3$^1/_2$oz)

15g ($^1/_2$oz) butter

sea salt

squeeze of lemon juice to taste

TO SERVE

20 chervil sprigs

2 sheets gold leaf (optional)

◆ Yabbies are my favourite crustacean—they are sweet and juicy and lend themselves to many preparations. Here I pair them with a risotto. There are many theories on making the best risotto. My father taught me as a boy the method used in Switzerland and northern Italy—not only is it the easiest method but it turns out perfect results time after time. A good risotto should be soupy in texture. To counter the richness of the Milanese risotto, a sauvignon blanc would be a good match.

FOR THE RISOTTO ALLA MILANESE: Heat the olive oil and half the butter in a stainless steel pan. Sweat the shallots until soft—do not allow them to colour. Add the rice and saffron and stir well. Add the hot chicken stock and the remaining tablespoon of butter, cover the pan, and turn down to a slow simmer for 15 minutes. Check the risotto and stir, adding a little more stock if needed, and continue cooking for a further 5 minutes or until the rice is al dente. Remove from the heat and stir in the grated fontina cheese and the bone marrow (if used) until they have melted and amalgamated.

FOR THE YABBIES: Plunge the yabbies into a pot of rapidly boiling salted water and then turn it off. Leave them for 2–3 minutes and drain. Peel off the shells and toss the yabbies in the butter. Season with sea salt and a squeeze of lemon juice.

TO SERVE: Spoon the risotto into a shallow serving bowl, arrange the yabbies on top and garnish with gold leaf and chervil sprigs.

MAKES 4 SERVINGS

Israeli Couscous Cooked Like a Paella, Shellfish, Crisp Chicken Wings

CHICKEN WINGS

50g (1³/₄oz) crushed sea salt

8 coriander seeds, crushed

1tsp cinnamon powder

zest of 1 orange

1tsp garlic powder

8 chicken wings, tips removed

500ml (17¹/₂fl oz) duck or goose fat,
 rendered

COUSCOUS PAELLA

1 onion, finely chopped

50ml (1³/₄fl oz) olive oil

250g (9oz) Israeli couscous

2tsp sweet smoked paprika

¹/₂tsp saffron powder

350ml (12fl oz) chicken stock

SHELLFISH GARNISH

125ml (4¹/₂fl oz) dry white wine

12 black mussels, cleaned

8 raw yabbies

1Tbsp butter

juice of 1 lemon

1 chorizo sausage, diced

1 tube calamari, cleaned and diced

TO COMPLETE

150g (5oz) frozen peas

3 tomatoes, blanched, peeled and diced

80ml (2¹/₂fl oz) crustacean veloute (see
 recipe, page 261)

1tsp chopped chives

8 chervil sprigs

◆ This dish is a fun play on paella using Israeli couscous instead of rice. A good wine match would be a Margaret River semillon/sauvignon blanc blend or a nice sancerre from the Loire Valley.

FOR THE CHICKEN WINGS: Mix together the salt, coriander seeds, cinnamon, orange zest and garlic powder. Toss the chicken wings in this mixture, rubbing the spices in well. Leave in the refrigerator covered with clingfilm for about 3 hours.

Preheat the oven to 120°C (250°F). Set the rendered duck or goose fat in an ovenproof pan and melt in the heated oven. Wash the chicken wings under cold running water and dry well. Gently place them in the warm duck fat, cover and return to the oven for about 2½ hours, until the wing bones are easily removed from the wings.

Remove the chicken wings from the fat and allow them to cool sufficiently so you can handle them. Carefully slide out the bones and cartilage, trying to maintain the shape of the wing. Place on a tray lined with greaseproof paper, cover with a second sheet of greaseproof paper and place another tray on top. Lightly weight this tray to press the chicken wings. Refrigerate until ready to use.

The duck fat may be strained and re-used.

CONTINUES ON PAGE 69

FOR THE COUSCOUS PAELLA: In a saucepan, gently sweat the onions in the olive oil without colouring. Add the couscous, paprika and saffron powders, stir and add the hot stock. Bring to the boil and then simmer very gently for about 10 minutes, until the couscous is cooked. Cool on a tray if not using immediately.

FOR THE SHELLFISH GARNISH: Bring the white wine to the boil in a stainless steel pan and throw in the yabbies and mussels. Cover and steam for 3–5 minutes, until the mussels have opened. Drain. Peel the yabbies and toss them in a little butter and a squeeze of lemon juice. Leave the mussels in the shell.

Meanwhile, heat a frying pan and sauté the chorizo. When it is nicely browned, add the calamari and toss very quickly a couple of times, squeeze in some lemon juice and drain into a colander.

TO COMPLETE: Sauté the chicken wings in a heavy-based pan until the skin is crisp—do not season as they will be salty enough already. Reheat the couscous with a little more stock, correct the seasoning and add the peas and diced tomatoes. Spoon some couscous into a shallow bowl or small copper pan and top with the chicken wings, shellfish and chorizo. Froth up the shellfish veloute with a handheld blender and spoon some over the dish. Sprinkle with chopped chives and garnish with chervil sprigs.

MAKES 4 SERVINGS

Seared Yamba Prawn Tail, Garlic Butter, Parsley, Lemon, Croutons

PARSLEY COULIS

6 shallots, sliced

30g (1oz) butter

20ml (²/₃fl oz) Pernod

100ml (3¹/₂fl oz) champagne veloute (see recipe, page 261)

50g (1³/₄oz) cooked spinach, drained and chopped

100g (3¹/₂oz) curly parsley, chopped

GARLIC BEURRE NOISETTE

100g (3¹/₂oz) butter

3 cloves garlic, crushed

20ml (²/₃fl oz) lemon juice

1 lemon, peeled, segmented and diced

1 tomato, peeled, seeded and diced

SEARED PRAWNS

12 medium to large raw prawns

garlic oil

squeeze of lemon juice

sea salt

TO SERVE

2Tbsp mini croutons, fried in butter (see recipe, page 265)

micro parsley

◆ The Hawkesbury used to be famous for its prawns but it is mostly little 'schoolies' that are now caught in the river. We get our large prawns from the north coast around Yamba and they are sweet and delicate. This dish is a variation on the garlic prawn. A nice New World chardonnay would match this best, or a semillon.

FOR THE PARSLEY COULIS: Sweat the shallots in the butter without colouring them. Add the Pernod and reduce by half and then add the champagne veloute. Bring to the boil and add the spinach and parsley. Simmer for 5 minutes and then blend to a smooth puree.

FOR THE GARLIC BEURRE NOISETTE: Heat the butter in a non-reactive pan with the crushed garlic cloves until the butter solids start colouring. When the butter is foaming and a nut brown colour, add the lemon juice, remove from the heat and strain through a coffee or oil filter. Add the diced lemon and tomato and keep warm.

FOR THE SEARED PRAWNS: Peel the prawns, leaving the tails attached. Slice down the back of each prawn and remove the intestinal tract. Continue slicing through the prawn without cutting through completely, then you can butterfly the tail out. Lay the prawns on a tray and brush with the garlic oil and then blast them with a blowtorch until they start to curl up. Season with lemon juice and sea salt.

TO SERVE: Spoon some of the parsley puree onto each plate and top with the seared prawn tails, add the lemon and tomato to the garlic beurre noisette and spoon over the prawns and sprinkle with the fried mini croutons and micro parsley.

MAKES 4 SERVINGS

Mud Crab Mezzaluna, Native Pepper Paste, Sweetcorn

MUD CRAB MEZZALUNA

20g (^{2}/$_3$oz) native pepper paste (see recipe,
    page 258)
30ml (1fl oz) mayonnaise (see recipe,
    page 263)
juice of 1 lemon
200g (7oz) mud crab meat, carefully picked
    to remove all the shell
12 round gyoza wrappers
1 egg white

SWEETCORN

6 shallots, finely chopped
30g (1oz) butter
^{1}/$_2$tsp saffron powder
1 x 420g (14oz) tin sweetcorn kernels in brine
200ml (7fl oz) chicken stock
50ml (1^3/$_4$fl oz) cream

TO COMPLETE

40g (1^1/$_2$oz) butter
squeeze of lemon juice
100g (3^1/$_2$oz) baby spinach leaves

◆ Mud crabs run a close second to yabbies as my favourite crustacean and so was delighted when I realised we could catch 2 kilograms (4lb 6oz) right off our pontoon at the Inn! This dish is a play on my favourite Singaporean dish of black pepper crab. My wine suggestion would be a chablis or unwooded chardonnay.

FOR THE MUD CRAB MEZZALUNA: Mix the pepper paste and mayonnaise with the lemon juice in a bowl and gently fold in the mud crab meat. Lay out the 12 gyoza wrappers on a bench. Place a spoonful of crab meat in the centre of each wrapper, brush the wrapper edges with egg white and fold over to form a mezzaluna or half-moon shape. Seal the mezzaluna and make sure that there is no air trapped inside. Keep in the refrigerator covered with a dry tea towel until they are needed.

FOR THE SWEETCORN: Sweat the shallots in half the butter until soft but not coloured. Add the saffron powder and then the sweetcorn and its brine. Bring to the boil and add the chicken stock. Cook until the stock has reduced by half and then add the cream. Simmer for a few minutes. Strain the liquid into a clean pan (reserving the sweetcorn and shallots), return to the stove and bring back to the boil. Whisk in the remaining butter and season with sea salt and lemon juice, then strain again. Keep the sauce warm.

Meanwhile, blend the sweetcorn and shallots until you have a smooth puree. Correct seasoning with sea salt and a squeeze of lemon juice.

TO COMPLETE: Cook the mezzaluna in plenty of boiling salted water until they float. Remove and toss in half the butter and the lemon juice. In a pan over moderate heat, toss the spinach in the rest of the butter and season with sea salt; when wilted, drain and arrange on the plates. Spoon over some sweetcorn puree and top with the mezzaluna. Foam up the sauce with a blender and spoon a little over the mezzaluna.

MAKES 4 SERVINGS

Grilled Sea Scallops, Cauliflower Puree, Tapenade, Green Apple Reduction

CAULIFLOWER PUREE

400g (14oz) cauliflower florets

80g (2$\frac{1}{2}$oz) shallots, peeled

200ml (7fl oz) chicken stock

100ml (3$\frac{1}{2}$fl oz) milk

APPLE REDUCTION

200ml (7fl oz) apple juice, unsweetened

20ml ($\frac{2}{3}$fl oz) lemon juice

THE SCALLOPS

12 sea scallops

50g (1$\frac{1}{2}$oz) butter, softened

juice of 1 lemon

sea salt

freshly ground whie pepper

TO SERVE

20g ($\frac{2}{3}$oz) tapenade (see recipe, page 263)

15g ($\frac{1}{2}$oz) chives, finely chopped

4 chervil sprigs

◆ This became a 'signature' dish at Forty One. Here we use the wonderful sea scallops from Queensland but any scallops will work. They are matched with the sweet (cauliflower), the salty (olives) and the sour (apple reduction) to produce a perfect foil for these beautiful, barely cooked scallops. A crisp reisling would be my choice to complement the dish.

FOR THE CAULIFLOWER PUREE: Sweat the shallots in a little butter and add the cauliflower. Half-cover with warm chicken stock and then top up with milk. Bring to the boil and simmer until the cauliflower is tender. Drain. Puree the cauliflower in a blender. The puree may be kept warm if using immediately or allowed to chill for later use.

FOR THE APPLE REDUCTION: Place the apple and lemon juices in a non-reactive saucepan and bring to the boil. Reduce until a syrupy consistency is left in the pan.

FOR THE SCALLOPS: Preheat a grill to very hot. Brush the scallops with soft butter and place on the heated grill. After 30 seconds, turn once at right angles. Leave for another 30 seconds and then turn the scallops over and repeat the process. Remove the scallops from the grill and squeeze over some lemon juice. Season with seaweed salt if you have it, or sea salt, and a grind of white pepper.

TO SERVE: Place 3 spoonfuls of cauliflower puree on a plate and place a seared scallop on top of each. Place a small quenelle of tapenade beside them. Drizzle the scallops and tapenade with the green apple reduction. Sprinkle the chopped chives on each of the scallops and a sprig of chervil on the tapenade.

MAKES 4 SERVINGS

4

TABLE COURSE

The history of the Inn—my first impressions

I passed through Sydney in the early 1980s and on that first visit to Australia my very first meal was at Berowra Waters Inn. We had arrived that afternoon on a flight from Auckland and, after checking into our hotel, had taken the hire car and a map and headed off to the 'bush' to visit this restaurant I had read about in the food journals and magazines of the day.

We had a booking for 7.30 for dinner but the journey was faster than I had anticipated. We were heading down through the Berowra regional park just before 7PM. It was a balmy summer's night in January and the cicadas were in full chorus. I parked under a gumtree on a dirt road, following the directions I had been given.

Anticipating a fine dining experience, we had dressed for the occasion and the rather warm evening was already making me uncomfortable about my choice of attire. After several minutes of searching, I discovered a sign overgrown with native bush. It pointed down some concrete steps to a pontoon, which contained a couple of fishermen and little else.

In one of life's 'six degrees of separation' moments, I realised I knew one of the fishermen, a young Maori lad called Reece who had been one of my apprentices a couple of years earlier in New Zealand.

Reece confirmed we were in the right spot and that the Inn was just around the river bend. This was confirmed several minutes later when another car arrived with similarly overdressed

people, who proceeded to wait and perspire on the pontoon with us.

By the time we had reached our reservation time, there were a couple of dozen guests on the pontoon and stretching up the steps to the track. At a quarter to eight the number had swelled to almost 40 well-heeled patrons. Shortly a small ferry rounded the river bend and plodded across to the landing without a care in the world. Only capable of taking 12 or so guests at a time, the ensuing rush was a polite version of a breakdown in rugby.

Being first on the pontoon, we were able to secure a place on the first ferry. We headed downstream and to my first meal at the Inn. I immediately fell in love with the location and with the sandstone and glass-louvred building on the banks of the river. Its simplicity and location reminded me of the alpine chalets and mountain pastures of my childhood, not because of its look but its aesthetics, its serenity, its simplicity and the rugged remoteness of the place. While dining I fantasisied, as young chefs tend to, of what I would do with the restaurant if it were mine.

It only took until 2007, 25 years later, for that dream to became a reality—although it nearly had in 1995. My Sydney restaurant Forty One had only been open a couple of years and was breaking records weekly when Gay Bilson decided to sell the Inn. I was very excited at the idea of buying it, but in the end the demands of Forty One, plus the potential stress of taking on Australia's most established and awarded

restaurant of the time, straight after Gay and chef Janni Kyritsis had departed, seemed a foolish idea.

So, in 2006, when my general manager at Forty One casually remarked that he'd read a piece in the *Sydney Morning Herald* about the Inn being available again, my interest was immediately piqued. The wheels starting turning. And this time the dream became a reality.

On restaurant reservations

The restaurant experience begins the moment you start making your reservation and it doesn't finish until the meal is a distant memory. When dining at good restaurants, a reservation is usually essential— and for an excellent reason.

Good food and good service are not matters of chance. A lot of time, effort and thought goes into the whole production. If every guest arrives at the same time, or twice as many guests arrive as were planned for, then even the best restaurant will struggle.

And the reason why a restaurant needs to confirm a booking for a particular service is that it wants to survive, to flourish—to make the restaurant even better. If people book and then don't show up, it can often be the difference between profit and loss for the evening in an industry where profit margins at the top end in small restaurants are usually in single digits.

All good restaurants try to stagger their bookings for the simple reason that if everyone turned up at once the level of food and service would either decline or the wait would be intolerable. I find it amazing that often diners do not understand this simple concept. After all, they are coming to the restaurant because of its reputation and yet, right from the first moment, they are trying to stop us doing our best. Chefs and restauranteurs in general love to give good service, to show generosity, to take the art of hospitality to its zenith, and it can be frustrating when the very

SEARED KANGAROO CARPACCIO

people we want to care for are the ones making it difficult for us to do so.

For some bizarre reason, diners often treat restaurants differently to other businesses. They would never book an appointment at two different doctors and then decide at the last minute which to visit —and not even have the courtesy to cancel the other one. They would never buy four tickets to the ballet and turn up as a party of six and demand to be let in. They would never arrive late for a movie and expect the cinema to speed up the movie so they could leave on time. It is a constant source of amazement to me, particularly in these days of mobile phones, that guests who have decided for whatever reason not to come to the restaurant seem incapable of calling to let us know. Even though we reconfirm bookings on the day, we still get occasional no-shows. In my younger days I would wait until the restaurant was closing at 1.30 in the morning and then ring the guest to ask whether they were joining us or should I let the staff go home!

Tart Tatin of Lemon Shallots, Goat's Cheese Fondue, Wild Rocket

TART TATIN

20g ($^2/_3$oz) butter

16 large lemon shallots (see recipe, page 264)

4 x 8cm discs puff pastry (see recipe, page 266)

2 egg yolks

GOAT'S CHEESE FONDUE

100ml (3$^1/_2$fl oz) sauvignon blanc

100ml (3$^1/_2$fl oz) cream

150g (5oz) fresh soft goat's cheese

TO SERVE

100g (3$^1/_2$oz) wild rocket leaves

20g ($^2/_3$oz) shallot, finely diced

20ml ($^2/_3$fl oz) aged balsamic vinegar

60ml (2fl oz) extra virgin olive oil

20g ($^2/_3$oz) kalamata olive, finely diced

16 long chives

FOR THE TART TATIN: Preheat the oven to 150°C. Brush four 6cm non-stick tart moulds with butter and arrange the cooked lemon shallots in each. Brush the puff pastry discs with the egg yolk and place over the shallots, tucking them in tightly. Brush the top of the pastry with egg yolk and leave in the refrigerator for 15 minutes. Bake in the heated oven for 15 minutes until the pastry is cooked. Rest for 5 minutes before unmoulding.

FOR THE GOAT'S CHEESE FONDUE: Pour the wine into a non-reactive pan and reduce by three-quarters over medium heat, add the cream and bring back to the boil. Break up the goat's cheese and whisk into the boiling cream until it melts.

TO SERVE: Spoon some of the goat's cheese fondue onto each plate and place a tart tatin, shallot side up, in the middle of each pool of fondue. Toss the rocket leaves with the shallots, aged balsamic vinegar and olive oil. Toss together and season with sea salt. Place a thatch of salad leaves on each tart and sprinkle with the olives and chives.

MAKES 4 SERVINGS

Spaetzli Noodles, Organic Egg Yolk, Baby Spinach, Fresh Winter Truffles

SPAETZLI NOODLES

1tsp sea salt

500g (17^1/$_2$oz) 00 flour

4 organic eggs

1Tbsp cream

125ml (4^1/$_2$fl oz) water

125ml (4^1/$_2$fl oz) milk

50g (1^3/$_4$oz) butter

THE EGGS

4 organic eggs

TO COMPLETE

8 shallots, sliced

50g (1^3/$_4$oz) butter

sea salt

200g (7oz) baby spinach leaves

50g (1^3/$_4$oz) fontina cheese, grated

20g (^{2}/$_3$oz) fresh truffle

1tsp chopped chives

◆ I grew up on spaetzli—I still love nothing better than a bowl of spaetzli baked in the oven with local mountain cheese and fried onions. I have dressed it up a bit with poached eggs and fresh truffles. Traditionally, spaetzli is made by flicking the dough from a wooden board into the boiling water but this takes some practice so I suggest an easier method. The best wine with this would be a gamay or pinot noir.

FOR THE SPAETZLI NOODLES: On a bench, add the sea salt to the flour and make a well in the centre. Whisk the eggs and cream together. Mix the water and milk. Pour the egg-cream mixture into the well in the flour and start incorporating the flour, adding enough of the milk-water mixture to make a soft dough that is slightly firmer than thick paste. Holding the bowl firmly in one hand, use the other hand to 'beat' the paste, lifting it into the air to work the gluten in the flour and aerate the dough.

To cook the noodles, bring a pot of salted water to the boil. Hold a colander with large holes above the pot. Put the dough into the colander, then gently press it through the holes using a pastry scraper— the spaetzli will drop into the water below. While the spaetzli are cooking, brown the 50g (1¾oz) butter in a pan. As the spaeztli rise to the surface, lift them out with a sieve and toss in the browned butter.

FOR THE EGGS: Preheat the oven to 65°C (150°F). Place a pan of water in the heated oven. Put in 4 eggs in their shells and leave for 1 hour. Then gently break the shells and take out the eggs. The whites will be delicately set like a custard and the yolks should still be orange and bright.

TO COMPLETE: Sauté the shallots in the butter until they are golden, season with sea salt and remove from the pan. Using the same pan, wilt the spinach, then toss it with the shallots, spaeztli and the grated fontina cheese. Arrange the spaetzli in four shallow serving bowls and place a poached egg on top. Finely shave the fresh truffle over the dishes and sprinkle with chopped chives.

MAKES 4 SERVINGS

Butter-poached White Asparagus, Quail Egg Croustillant, Watercress

WHITE ASPARAGUS

12 spears jumbo white asparagus

50ml (1³/₄fl oz) milk

2tsp butter, plus a little for warming

¹/₄tsp sea salt

¹/₄tsp sugar

QUAIL EGG CROUSTILLANT

8 quail eggs

1 hen's egg

1Tbsp cream

50g (1³/₄oz) seasoned flour

100g (3¹/₂oz) fine white breadcrumbs

WATERCRESS

100ml (3¹/₂fl oz) champagne veloute

 (see recipe, page 261)

100g (3¹/₂oz) picked watercress leaves

100g (3¹/₂oz) baby spinach leaves

sea salt

TO COMPLETE

grapeseed oil for deep-frying

sea salt

50g (1³/₄oz) watercress

20ml (²/₃fl oz) French vinaigrette dressing

 (see recipe, page 262)

◆ We cook white asparagus *sous-vide* (see page 186) to maintain its great depth of flavour. It can be bitter, which is why we cook it with milk and sugar initially. Chardonnay would match this dish best.

FOR THE WHITE ASPARAGUS: Peel the asparagus spears and trim them to about 10cm (4in) in length. Line them up in a single layer in a vacuum pouch. Heat the milk and butter and dissolve the salt and sugar in it. Add to the pouch and seal it on medium high. Cook the asparagus in a water bath at 85°C for 30 minutes until tender and then submerge the bag immediately in ice water to chill. When ready to use, remove the asparagus from the vacuum bag and rinse quickly in cold water.

FOR THE QUAIL EGG CROUSTILLANT: Bring a pot of water to the boil and boil the quail eggs for 2 minutes. Immediately refresh them in ice water and gently peel them, keeping the eggs whole and unbroken. Beat the hen's egg yolk with the cream. Gently toss the eggs in the seasoned flour and then dip them in the beaten egg yolk mixture. Drain, then dip them in the breadcrumbs, ensuring that you fully coat the egg in the breadcrumbs. Set aside until ready to serve.

FOR THE WATERCRESS: Bring the veloute to the boil, add the watercress and spinach, and cook until wilted. Drain. Blend until smooth. Add a little veloute if needed. Correct the seasoning with sea salt.

TO COMPLETE: Fry the quail eggs in hot oil (185°C/365°F) until golden, then season with sea salt. With a serrated knife, slice the tops off the eggs. Toss the asparagus in a pan with a little butter to warm through. Spoon some of the watercress puree onto the serving plate and arrange the warm asparagus on top. Garnish with the quail eggs and watercress tossed in French dressing. Decorate with a little more dressing.

MAKES 4 SERVINGS

Buffalo Ricotta Spinach Ravioli, Sage Butter, Wood Mushrooms

RICOTTA SPINACH RAVIOLI

50g (1³/₄oz) shallots, finely diced

butter

150g (5oz) fresh ricotta

150g (5oz) cooked spinach, drained and
    finely chopped

sea salt

freshly ground white pepper

12 gyoza or won ton wrappers

1 egg white

SAGE BUTTER

200g (7oz) unsalted butter

1 small bunch sage

juice of 1 lemon

1tsp chopped chives

1Tbsp diced tomato

MUSHROOMS

200g (7oz) mixed wood mushrooms,

50g (1³/₄oz) butter

50g (1³/₄oz) shallot confit (see recipe,
    page 264)

75ml (2¹/₂fl oz) chicken stock

TO COMPLETE

knob of butter

mini croutons (see recipe, page 265)

◆   Wood mushrooms are wonderful in autumn and we make a lovely vegetarian dish matching the earthy wood mushrooms with spinach and ricotta. Use fresh spinach if you can but frozen is a quick and easy substitute. This dish is ideal with either a full-bodied chardonnay or a light red.

FOR THE RICOTTA SPINACH RAVIOLI: Gently sweat the shallots in a little butter and remove from the pan. When cool add the ricotta and spinach. Mix together gently so you don't break down the ricotta too much and season well. Lay out half the gyoza wrappers and brush with a little egg white. Spoon the ricotta mix onto each gyoza wrapper and then fold in half to form a mezzaluna or half-moon shape. Seal well, expelling all the air and store on a dry tray until needed.

FOR THE SAGE BUTTER: Heat the butter in a stainless steel pan until it is a nut brown colour, add the chopped sage and lemon juice, remove from the stove and pass through a coffee or oil filter. Put the diced tomato and chopped chives in the butter and keep warm.

FOR THE MUSHROOMS: Saute the mushrooms in the butter, season with sea salt, and add the shallot confit and chicken stock. Cook until reduced and the mushrooms are nicely glazed.

TO COMPLETE: Cook the ravioli in plenty of boiling salted water until they float to the top, about 2 minutes. Drain and toss with a knob of butter. Arrange the ravioli in serving bowls, top with the mushrooms and sage butter, and sprinkle with mini croutons.

MAKES 4 SERVINGS

Spaghettini 'En Papillote' with Rocket, Wild Mushrooms, Garlic and Chilli Oil

200g (7oz) spaghettini, cooked and refreshed
   in ice water
30ml (1fl oz) chilli oil (see recipe, page 258)
sea salt
100g (3^1/$_2$oz) garlic butter (see recipe,
   page 259)
100g (3^1/$_2$oz) shiitake mushrooms
100g (3^1/$_2$oz) chanterelle mushrooms

100g (3^1/$_2$oz) porcini or cep mushrooms
40g (1^1/$_2$oz) shallot confit, finely diced (see
   recipe, page 264)
50ml (1^3/$_4$fl oz) chicken stock
120g (4oz) rocket
50g (1^3/$_4$oz) enoki mushrooms
16 slices red chilli
juice of 1 lemon

◆ This is a dish that I developed for Singapore Airlines while I was a consultant for the company. Using an old technique of cooking 'en papillote', it makes a fun and interesting way to serve a pasta dish. The best wine to drink with it would be a chablis, chardonnay or semillon.

FOR THE PAPILLOTE: Cut a large heart-shaped piece of silicone or baking paper for each portion, approximately 25cm (10in) across. In a bowl toss together the spaghettini and chilli oil and season to taste with some sea salt. Heat half the garlic butter in a pan and add all the mushrooms except the enoki. Sauté quickly just to half-cook the mushrooms, then add the shallot confit and chicken stock and toss well. Reduce the stock quickly, remove the mushrooms from the heat and leave to cool.

Lay out the paper sheets and divide the pasta between them, positioning it on one half of the heart shape. Top with the sautéed mushrooms, the rocket leaves, then the enoki, then a slice of garlic butter and 3 slices of red chilli. Fold the other side of the heart shape over the filling and, starting at the wide end, fold over the edges of the paper in small tucks all the way around, so the parcel is sealed tightly (see illustrations on page 266).

TO COMPLETE: Preheat the oven to 200°C. Place the papillotes on a tray and bake for 5 to 6 minutes. The bags will brown slightly and puff up. Serve immediately so your guests can open their own papillote.

MAKES 4 SERVINGS

5 THE

FISH COURSE

On how to use a good restaurant

Years of experience and hard work will have gone into creating a successful fine dining restaurant. Especially where the chef is the owner, it reflects a total commitment. It is the sum of its parts—the skill, dedication, hard work and training of the chef; the extensive thought and deliberation over the tiniest details; the procurement of the finest ingredients, tableware, linen, wines and stemware. If an item appears on the menu, then that item will be in season and of the highest quality the restaurant can procure. The dish will have been created incorporating ingredients to accentuate and compliment the main component—so when a diner asks for it 'without the sauce', it would be like having a great ballet without the music: you could watch it but it would not be the same.

The major disadvantage of 'à la carte' is that most diners have no idea how to construct a balanced menu. Like all my colleagues, over the years I have had guests who phone the next day to announce they have 'food poisoning' … upon closer investigation we discover that they ordered Blini of Scampi with a Champagne Caviar Veloute, followed by the Venison Wellington, Sauce Albufera (a foie gras-enriched cream sauce) and Chocolate Tart, Raspberries and White Chocolate Cream. Three dishes all containing heavy doses of cream, accompanied by a few bottles of red wine, after one or two cream-based cocktails. Now they are unwell and have 'food poisoning'!

To get the best out of a restaurant requires an attitude of trust on the part of the diners. Like all top restaurants, we enjoy hosting our guests, we love to welcome them, to make them smile, to enhance their shared experience. We are in the business of selling memories—food can be obtained anywhere but we want our guests to depart with memories that will last the test of time, and if they don't we have failed. To enable us to do this, diners need to trust that a lot of thought and professionalism have gone into the 'experience'—and just let us do what we do.

When ordering, the best option is to ask the chef to pick the dishes. In a good restaurant, the chef will

want to impress and he'll select what he considers the best of the evening's menu. That simple request immediately gives your order status—there is a serious diner, an appreciative audience, among the dockets on the board—so it rises above the others as it now has personality and the chef has taken responsibility for it.

While all diners are created equal, some are definitely more equal than others. In a good restaurant you should get a very good meal and service as a base minimum—but how much better it gets than that very often depends on the guests themselves. Distinguishing yourself above other diners will get the best results. Making your table a pleasure to serve will always result in better service than that received by guests who are rude or condescending. Idiosyncrasies are good as well … order a dry martini with extra olives, eat the olives and tell the waiter you are finished. This will put you into the special category. We have two regular diners who arrive with some stuffed toys that they proceed to set up at the table to join them for lunch. That goes into the special category too. Phoning ahead and leaving a message for yourself to 'call the PM's office on the private number' will obviously get the waiter's attention. The old trick of getting out a notebook and scribbling furiously when tasting the food no longer works … chances are the scribbler is a 'foodie' and not a restaurant critic—and no waiter or chef really likes self-confessed foodies.

Thoughts on fish

When asked in interviews, 'what is your favourite thing to cook', most chefs answer … 'Fish'.

It is up there as a standard chef answer, along with 'my mother was a great cook and she inspired me' and 'I started as a pot wash and worked my way up'—neither of which really applies to me, although my mother is a very good cook.

So why the answer fish? Well, fish is the most versatile of all proteins, it has a great variety of flavours and textures, it adapts well to all styles of cooking and is the best centrepiece for an endless variety of garnishes and sauces. It is lighter and healthier than meat and it lends itself to better presentation.

The most important thing with fish, like all other ingredients, is its quality. Unfortunately, fish is often mistreated, it isn't handled correctly, it bruises easily and, if not properly iced and transported, deteriorates quickly. If you are storing fish, do so in plenty of ice

and make sure the melted ice can drain off so the fish doesn't end up in a pool of water, which can damage its flesh. Fresh fish should have clear protruding eyes and its skin and flesh should be firm and spring back when you touch it. Most importantly, it should smell fresh and of the sea.

Fifty years ago the coastal seas were fished up to a depth of only around 50 metres (160 feet) but nowadays, with deep-sea long-line fishing and gill nets, fishermen cover the entire oceans to depths of over 250 metres (820 feet). This is effectively raping the seas of stock and causing unknown damage to the maritime ecosystem. It is important that we establish a sustainable balance in our harvesting of wild fish to avoid the possibilities of certain species becoming extinct in the near future.

Australia has several well-established aquaculture farms and we regularly feature their fish on our menus. My particular favourites are murray cod—this is better than the wild fish, which being freshwater has a tendancy to taste 'muddy'—stunning kingfish and suzuki mulloway from South Australia and ocean trout and salmon from Tasmania. Work is progressing in the Kimberley region of Western Australia, which has an outstanding biological and natural resource base for aquaculture, including year-round warm waters. They are experimenting with the farming of such species as red emperor, grouper, coral trout, mud crabs, pearl oysters and abalone. The time is not too far away when we will be able to cook a great variety of fish and shellfish that are purely farmed and give the oceans a chance to heal themselves.

SLOW-COOKED OCEAN TROUT

Fillet of Murray Cod, Hawkesbury Calamari, Cauliflower, Minced Olives

MURRAY COD

4 x 100g (3¹/₂oz) murray cod fillets, boned,
　　skin on
50g (1³/₄oz) butter
juice of 1 lemon
sea salt

CALAMARI

2tsp plain flour
1tsp sweet paprika
1tsp sea salt
320g (11oz) Hawkesbury calamari, cleaned

grapeseed oil for deep-frying

TO COMPLETE

100g (3¹/₂oz) cauliflower puree (see recipe,
　　page 75)
knob of butter
50g (1³/₄oz) tapenade (see recipe, page 263)
2tsp chopped chives
1tsp finely diced red chilli
50ml (1³/₄fl oz) lemon-infused extra virgin
　　olive oil
20g (²/₃oz) micro dill

◆ The Hawkesbury is famous for its calamari and we always try to have a dish featuring it. Here we have married the calamari with murray cod, which is a beautiful delicate farmed fish. The dish is best suited to a full-bodied chardonnay.

FOR THE MURRAY COD: Heat a heavy-based frying pan. Brush the skin side of the cod with butter and place it, skin side down, in the pan. Cook until the top side of the flesh starts to go opaque, then turn the fish over, add the rest of the butter and let it foam, then squeeze over the lemon juice. Immediately remove the pan from the stove and let the fish sit for a moment. Season with sea salt.

FOR THE CALAMARI: Mix together the flour, paprika and sea salt. Open out the calamari tubes by slicing down one side with a sharp knife. Scrape the inside of the tube and then cut in half lengthways. In a deep-fryer, heat some grapeseed oil to 180°C (350°F). Toss the calamari in the seasoned flour, then plunge into the hot oil for about 60 seconds. Remove and slice into rounds (the calamari will have curled up).

TO COMPLETE: Reheat the cauliflower puree with a knob of butter. Spoon some of the puree onto each serving plate and arrange the murray cod on top. Sprinkle the sliced calamari around the plate and dot some of the tapenade around. Mix together the chopped chives, chilli and lemon oil and drizzle around the plate. Garnish with the micro dill.

MAKES 4 SERVINGS

Yellowfin Tuna Pepper Steak,
Pommes Pont Neuf

POMMES PONT NEUF

1kg (2lb 3oz) maris piper or russet burbank
    potatoes, peeled

2L (70fl oz) grapeseed oil

sea salt

PEPPERED TUNA

400g (14oz) centre-cut yellowfin tuna,
    sashimi grade

40g (1¹/₂oz) native pepper paste (see recipe,
    page 258)

sea salt

100g (3¹/₂oz) butter

juice of 1 lemon

TO COMPLETE

200g (7oz) baby spinach leaves

50g (1³/₄oz) butter

sea salt

20g (²/₃oz) green peppercorns

2 tomatoes, peeled, seeded and diced

80ml pepper veloute (see recipe, page 262)

8 sprigs chervil

◆   While I usually prefer tuna raw, I make an exception in this case. The fragrant pepper paste makes the tuna ideal for this non-meat variation on a pepper steak and chips. Drink some pinot noir with it or even a zinfandel.

FOR THE *POMMES PONT NEUF*: Cut the potatoes into large 'pont neuf'-style chips (1 x 1 x 6cm/ ½ x ½ x 2½in). Wash the chips under running water for 2–3 minutes to remove excess starch. Bring a large pan of salted water to the boil and add the chips, bring back to the boil and simmer gently until they are cooked. Be careful that they do not break up. Carefully drain the chips and place on a rack to cool, then put in the refrigerator uncovered.

Heat the grapeseed oil to 130°C (266°F) and cook the chips until they are lightly coloured. Drain and cool on a rack again.

When you are ready to serve the chips, heat the oil to 190°C (374°F) and fry until golden brown, drain well and season with sea salt.

FOR THE PEPPERED TUNA: Cut the tuna into four 'steaks', brush with the pepper paste and leave to marinate for 30 minutes. Heat a heavy-based frying pan, season the tuna with sea salt and quickly sear in the hot pan, about 30 seconds each side. Add the butter and let it foam, then squeeze over the lemon juice.

TO COMPLETE: Wilt the spinach in the butter, season with sea salt and drain. Arrange on the serving plates. Sit the tuna on top of the spinach and garnish with green peppercorns and diced tomato. Warm the sauce, then foam it up with a handheld blender and spoon over the tuna. Serve the *pommes pont neuf* separately.

MAKES 4 SERVINGS

Fillet of Wild Barramundi, 'French Onion Soup' Puree, Peppered Oxtail Croustillant

4 pieces oxtail, about 1kg (2lb 3oz), from the
     thick part of the tail, trimmed of fat

sea salt

1 large onion, diced

1 large leek, sliced

2 cloves garlic, sliced

1 large field or portobello mushroom,
     sliced

2 sprigs fresh thyme

100ml (3^1/$_2$fl oz) madeira

1L (35fl oz) chicken stock

50g (1^1/$_2$oz) caramelised onions (see recipe,
     page 171)

1tsp native pepper paste (see recipe,
     page 258)

4 sheets Tunisian brik pastry

1 large egg white

2 large white onions, sliced

1 large pinch sea salt

1Tbsp butter

50ml (1^3/$_4$fl oz) sherry vinegar

100ml (3^1/$_2$fl oz) veal stock

100ml (3^1/$_2$fl oz) chicken stock

^{1}/$_2$tsp xanthum gum

4 x 100g (3^1/$_2$oz) wild barramundi fillets,
     boned, skin on

50g (1^1/$_2$oz) butter

juice of 1 lemon

80ml (2^1/$_2$fl oz) champagne veloute (see
     recipe, page 261)

20g (^{2}/$_3$oz) crème fraiche or sour cream

20g (^{2}/$_3$oz) micro coriander

◆   Wild barramundi is a beautiful fish found in Queensland and the Northern Territory, Australia's answer to sea bass. It is a meaty fish and can handle big flavours like the peppered oxtail croustillant, which by the way make a great entrée of its own or finger food for a cocktail party. This dish calls for a chilled gamay or pinot noir.

FOR THE PEPPERED OXTAIL CROUSTILLANT: Heat a heavy-based frying pan and sear the oxtail, giving it good colour, and season well with sea salt. Remove from the pan and place in *sous-vide* bag. Pour the excess fat from the pan and add the onions, leeks, garlic and mushrooms, sauté until soft and then deglaze with the madeira. When the madeira is reduced, add the stock and thyme sprigs. Simmer for 1 hour and then strain.

Add the stock to the meat in the *sous-vide* bag and seal in a vacuum machine. Cook in a water bath at 83°C for 8 hours, then remove the bags from the water bath and plunge into ice water to cool. When cool, remove the oxtail, reserving the stock, and strip the meat from the bones. Mix the meat

CONTINUES ON PAGE 108

with the caramelised onions and pepper paste. Correct seasoning with a touch of sea salt if needed. Lay the brik pastry sheets out on a bench and brush with egg white. Lay some of the peppered oxtail on the sheets and roll up to make four cigar-shaped pastries. Wrap the croustillants in clingfilm and refrigerate until ready to cook to stop them from drying out.

FOR THE 'FRENCH ONION SOUP' PUREE: Season the onions with the sea salt and gently sweat them in the butter until soft. Then increase the heat and keep cooking until the onions are a lovely even brown colour. Add the sherry vinegar and reduce to almost nothing, then add the two stocks and simmer the soup, uncovered, for 1 hour. Remove from the stove and add the xanthum gum. Pour the mixture into a blender and blitz for 3 minutes. Taste the puree and correct seasoning with sea salt if needed.

FOR THE WILD BARRAMUNDI: Heat a heavy-based saucepan. Brush the skin side of the barramundi with butter and place it, skin side down, in the pan. Cook until the top side of the flesh starts to go opaque. Turn the fish over, add the rest of the butter and let it foam, then squeeze over the lemon juice. Immediately remove the pan from the heat and let the fish sit for a moment. Season with sea salt.

TO COMPLETE: Sauté the oxtail croustillants in butter until golden brown and keep warm. Reheat the onion puree with a knob of butter. Smear the serving plates with the puree and arrange the barramundi on top. Slice the ends off the croustillant and lean against the fish. Heat the veloute, then add the crème fraiche and foam up with a handheld blender. Spoon some of the froth over the fish. Sprinkle with the micro coriander. Drizzle a few drops of aged balsamic around the fish.

MAKES 4 SERVINGS

Fillet of John Dory, Green Asparagus, Salted Grapes, Verjus

400g (14oz) grapes (large seedless white
   are best)

15g ($^1/_2$oz) sea salt

2tsp caster sugar

100ml (3$^1/_2$fl oz) olive oil

JOHN DORY

4 x 100g (3$^1/_2$oz) john dory fillets, boned,
   skin on

50g (1$^3/_4$oz) butter

juice of 1 lemon

sea salt

TO COMPLETE

200g (7oz) green asparagus, trimmed and
   peeled

50g (1$^3/_4$oz) butter

100ml (3$^1/_2$fl oz) verjus beurre blanc (see
   recipe, page 259)

20g ($^2/_3$oz) red amaranth

FOR THE SALTED GRAPES: Blanch the grapes in a pot of boiling water for 15 seconds and then plunge them into ice water. Drain and carefully peel the grapes, then lightly dry them. Mix together the salt and sugar and toss the grapes in the mixture. Place them in a dehydrator and dry until they lose half their volume and become wrinkly. Store in olive oil until needed.

FOR THE JOHN DORY: Heat a heavy-based pan, brush the skin of the john dory with butter and place it, skin down, in the pan. Cook until the flesh on the top side starts to go opaque, then turn the fish over. Add the rest of the butter to foam and squeeze over the lemon juice, and then immediately remove the pan from the stove and let the john dory sit for a moment. Season with sea salt.

TO COMPLETE: Cook the asparagus in boiling salted water, drain and toss in butter. Arrange the asparagus and the salted grapes on a plate and top with the John Dory fillets. Spoon over the verjus beurre blanc and garnish with the red amaranth.

MAKES 4 SERVINGS

Mulloway Fillet, Crab Croquette, Celeriac, Saltwater Pork Belly

CRAB CROQUETTE

100g (3^1/$_2$oz) crab meat, hand-picked

25g (^{3}/$_4$oz) ground almonds

10g (^{1}/$_3$oz) ham, finely diced (optional)

2tsp toasted fine white breadcrumbs

25g (^{3}/$_4$oz) walnut oil vinaigrette (see recipe, page 263)

25g (^{3}/$_4$oz) shallot confit, finely diced (see recipe, page 264)

seasoned flour

2 eggs, beaten with a little milk

200g (7oz) fine white breadcrumbs

CELERIAC PUREE

^{1}/$_2$ large white onion, sliced

^{1}/$_2$ clove garlic, sliced

150g (5oz) celeriac, diced

^{1}/$_2$tsp chicken stock powder

200ml (7oz) milk

75ml (2^1/$_2$fl oz) cream

knob of butter

sea salt

juice of ^{1}/$_2$ lemon

MULLOWAY

4 x 60g (2oz) mulloway fillets, boned, skin off

40ml (1^1/$_2$l oz) lemon-infused extra virgin olive oil

juice of 1 lemon

TO COMPLETE

120g (4oz) cooked pork belly (see recipe, page 172)

8 red radish tops

◆ I love seafood with meat and this is another example of how the sum of the parts are greater than the individual items. A chardonnay or semillon would be ideal with this dish.

FOR THE CRAB CROQUETTE: Mix together the first six ingredients and form into balls. Roll the croquettes in seasoned flour, dip into the beaten egg and then the breadcrumbs; roll so they are evenly coated with the breadcrumbs. Fry in a deep fryer at 180°C (350°F) until golden brown. Season with sea salt.

FOR THE CELERIAC PUREE: Sweat the onion and garlic without colouring. When soft, add the celeriac, chicken powder, milk and cream. Simmer until the celeriac is soft. Drain, reserving the cooking liquid. Puree the celeriac, using a little cooking liquid if needed for a smooth puree. Pour the puree onto a square of muslin, pull corners together and tie to form a 'sack'. Hang the muslin in the fridge over a bowl; drain for 12 hours. To reheat, place the puree in a pan with a knob of butter. Season with sea salt and lemon juice.

FOR THE MULLOWAY: With a sharp knife, score the top side of the mulloway with a criss-cross pattern. Using a blow torch, sear the top of the scored side and place the fillets in a sous-vide bag with the lemon-infused oil. Seal tightly in a vacuum machine and cook in a water bath at 62°C for 7 minutes.

TO COMPLETE: Roast the pork until skin is crisp; slice into four. Spoon some celeriac puree onto plates. Arrange the fish at one end of the puree, the crab croquette and pork at the other. Garnish with radish tops.

MAKES 4 SERVINGS

Slow-cooked Ocean Trout, Sweet Green Peas, Pig's Trotter, Smoked Eel

OCEAN TROUT

4 x 80g (2^1/$_2$oz) ocean trout, boned, skin on

sea salt

40ml (1^1/$_2$fl oz) extra virgin olive oil

100ml (3^1/$_2$fl oz) champagne veloute
  (see recipe, page 261)

50g (1^3/$_4$oz) smoked eel trimmings

1tsp lemon juice

SWEET GREEN PEAS

20g (^{2}/$_3$oz) shallots, finely diced

10g (^{1}/$_3$oz) butter

50ml (1^3/$_4$fl oz) cream

150g (5oz) frozen peas

sea salt

THE GARNISH

2 braised pig's trotters, sliced
  (see recipe, page 266)

30g (1oz) caramelised onions
  (see recipe, page 171)

100g (3^1/$_2$oz) smoked eel fillet

juice of ^{1}/$_2$ lemon

FOR THE OCEAN TROUT: Season the trout with sea salt and rub with extra virgin olive oil. Place the trout in a vacuum bag (or ziplock bag if you do not have a vacuum machine). Make sure the trout is at room temperature before cooking. Place the bagged trout in a pot of water on the stove. The water should not exceed 50°C (122°F). Cook very slowly for 5–10 minutes.

For the sauce, heat the champagne veloute and add the smoked eel trimmings, leave to infuse for 15 minutes and then pass through a fine sieve. Season with a squeeze of lemon juice and keep warm.

FOR THE SWEET GREEN PEAS: Sweat the finely diced shallots in the butter, add the cream and bring to the boil. Add the peas and some sea salt. As soon as it comes to the boil, remove the pan from the stove and blend the peas to a smooth puree. Cool on a tray in the refrigerator if you are not using at this stage; to reheat, just add a little knob of butter and heat gently in a pan.

FOR THE GARNISH: Sauté the pig's trotters until they are warm. Add the caramelised onions and cook until heated through. Just before removing from the heat, add the smoked eel and gently warm through. Taste for seasoning and add a squeeze of lemon juice.

TO COMPLETE: Place the warm pea puree on serving plates. Take the trout out of its bag, remove the skin, season and squeeze with lemon juice. Place it to the side of the puree and top the trout with the sautéed pig's trotter, smoked eel and pea shoots. Blitz the sauce with a handheld blender until light and frothy, spoon a little over the fish and serve.

MAKES 4 SERVINGS

SOUP COURSE

The history of the Inn—the later years

Gay and Tony Bilson purchased Berowra Waters in 1976. Tony had spent time on the Hawkesbury River as a child and loved the area. The couple commissioned the architect Glenn Murcutt to redesign the building. Respecting the Aboriginal philosophy of 'treading lightly on this earth', Glenn developed a glass 'verandah by the water' that remains the heart of the building today.

At Berowra Gay and Tony created Australia's first internationally recognised restaurant. In the early 1980s Tony left and was replaced in the kitchen by Janni Kyritsis, who with Gay continued to refine the restaurant through the rest of the decade.

By the mid-1990s the restaurant scene had changed dramatically and restaurants such as Forty One, Rockpool and Pier were well established in the city. The fact that Berowra Waters Inn had been successfully drawing diners in search of fine dining to the lower Hawkesbury River for 20 years was a great testament to those who had been part of the Bilson years at Berowra.

In 1995 Gay left Berowra to operate Bennelong restaurant at the Sydney Opera House with Janni as chef, and she leased the restaurant to Martin Teplitzky. The Berowra Waters property was sold after a couple of years and then in 2001 was bought by Jeremy Laws, initially as a holiday home. But, after researching the history of the Inn and realising its unique place in the history of Australian cuisine, he decided to reopen it as a restaurant and operated with some success until 2007.

In a last-ditch effort to breath life into the building and the restaurant he loved so much, Jeremy talked to the *Sydney Morning Herald*, which ran an article about him looking for someone to take over the operation of the restaurant. Coincidentally, I was at a turning point: Forty One Restaurant was 16 years old and there were only two years left on the lease. While I had enjoyed my time in the city, I was looking forward to a change. Berowra was the perfect next step—it would give me a dream location for my next restaurant. ... How could I resist?

On matching food and wine

You could fill books and websites with thoughts, theories and argument about food and wine matching and, indeed, many people have done so.

My philosophy is to drink what you enjoy and eat what you enjoy—and unless you are planning to have the food and the wine in your mouth at the same time it really doesn't matter.

But before the seekers of the holy grail of the perfect food and wine match take my book back to the shop for a refund, and ban me from gastronomic circles, I will get in quickly and say there certainly are wines—and other drinks—that do enhance or detract from the taste of particular foods.

There are millions of combinations that perfectly marry the style, flavours and textures of the food and the drink, whether by enhancing and complementing each other or by highlighting the differences.

I just wanted to establish that there are no hard and fast rules and you should never feel compelled to agree with palates other than your own. There are classic combinations, of course: chablis with oysters, pinot grigio and prosciutto, sauterne and foie gras, pinot noir and duck, and so on … and in each case the balance of the food and wine work together to make the whole greater than the sum of the parts.

In a gastronomic word association test, given the word 'champagne' most people will say 'caviar', and when prompted with 'caviar' they will come up with 'vodka'. This may sound as if some rich guy decided that if you have something expensive,

you should match it with something else that's expensive. This couldn't be further from the truth. What is interesting is that champagne is one of the only wines that truly stands up and complements the complex oily, fishy and salty flavours of caviar—a chablis or dry riesling might be acceptable but they are not in the same class. Vodka, on the other hand, totally changes the characteristics of the caviar, almost removing saltiness from the equation, and makes the slightly sweet fishy characteristics of the caviar prominent. Personally, I go for a compromise and add the vodka to the champagne before drinking it with my caviar.

Thoughts on soups

Soup is comfort food, the very essence of the ingredients that are distilled into a liquid for easy consumption. I have always enjoyed soups, from the rustic smoky ham and barley *gertsensuppe* and the *gulaschsuppe* (goulash soup) of my childhood to the refined consommés of fancy restaurants.

As a young chef I decided that each meal should have a soup course. Because diners back then were reluctant to order more than one entrée, I would serve everyone a small demitasse of soup before their last savoury course. This also had the advantage of filling in the time while the main course was prepared

to order. I thought I had created something unique, something special, only to find several months later when I visited Hong Kong that the Plume restaurant at the Regent Hotel had been doing this for years.

The demitasse of soup is something that I have served at all my restaurants since I worked in Hong Kong in the early 1980s. I love serving soup in these little cups. It is an explosion of flavour—just two or three sips of intense flavour.

Soup is very simple. You take the main ingredient, cook it perfectly, then puree it and adjust the consistency.

Cream soups are probably the easiest to master. If you ensure the base ingredient is of the best quality, then you almost cannot fail to produce a good soup. The liquid you use to convey the flavour depends on the ingredient. If it is a substantial vegetable such as potato or leek, then a good chicken stock is best. For a lighter vegetable like fresh garden peas, then a vegetable stock may be better. Adding a little cream adds body and texture, but too much will mute the flavours, and so it is best added at the end when you correct the seasoning.

Consommés are a thing of beauty, distilling the very essence of an ingredient, be it mushrooms or squabs or crabs, and then just highlighting it with a touch of tarragon or a drop of madeira. Making a consommé is an exacting process but it is so satisfying watching as the dense stock clarifies and the 'raft' of egg white successfully attracts all the impurities in the stock, leaving a crystal-clear liquid with an intense aroma and flavour.

Rustic soups like the *goulaschsoup* of my childhood are invariably winter soups, almost mini-stews or braises that can often substitute for a main course. A beautiful rich, warming hearty soup, some crusty bread, cold unsalted butter and a bottle of burgundy … what more could you want on a chilly winter's day? Although these are my favourite soups to eat with my family, we rarely make them in the restaurant because they tend to be a little too substantial. But it is fun to adapt them and, on more than one occasion, I have made a goulash consommé that has the intensity of the flavours of smoked paprika, beef and tomatoes but is a crystal-clear, dark red broth.

Oriental Duck Consommé, Roast Duck Sang Choi Bau

ORIENTAL DUCK STOCK

1 Chinese roast duck

2L (70fl oz) chicken stock

1 stalk lemongrass, chopped

1 onion, sliced

1 leek, washed and sliced

15g (1/2oz) fresh ginger, peeled and sliced

15g (1/2oz) galangal root, sliced

red chilli

3 star anise

50ml (1 3/4fl oz) ketjap manis soy sauce

25ml (3/4fl oz) dark superior soy sauce

50ml (1 3/4fl oz) Chinese oyster sauce

CONSOMMÉ CLARIFICATION

100g (3 1/2oz) minced chicken breast

6 egg whites

50ml (1 3/4fl oz) ketjap manis soy sauce

1 stalk lemongrass, finely chopped

3 kaffir lime leaves, chopped

1 cup mixed chopped herbs (basil, coriander and mint)

SANG CHOI BAU

2tsp pure roasted sesame oil

50g (1 3/4oz) carrot, julienned

50g (1 3/4oz) leek, julienned

50g (1 3/4oz) bean sprouts, cleaned

20ml (2/3oz) Chinese oyster sauce

meat from the duck, finely shredded

TO SERVE

8 sprigs coriander

4 iceberg lettuce leaves, each cut into a circle to form a cup

2tsp red chilli, finely diced

FOR THE ORIENTAL DUCK STOCK: Discard the duck skin. Take the meat off the bones and reserve. Chop up the carcass and place in a pot with the remaining stock ingredients. Slowly bring to the boil. Gently simmer for 3 hours, skimming the fat off the surface as it rises, and then pass through a fine sieve.

FOR THE CONSOMMÉ CLARIFICATION: Place the chicken, egg whites and soy sauce in a stainless steel saucepan and mix together well. Warm the stock slightly and pour it over the mixture, whisking well as you do so. Put the pan on the heat and bring to the boil slowly, stirring occasionally so that it doesn't stick and burn. When the solids float to the top and form a 'crust', make a small hole in the crust to stop it breaking apart and making the consommé cloudy. Simmer gently for another 30 minutes or so, until the particles stop floating to the top. Remove from the heat. Line a chinoise strainer with muslin and put in the chopped herbs and another layer of fine muslin. Carefully pass the consommé over the herbs. Discard the crust.

FOR THE SANG CHOI BAU: Heat a wok, add the sesame oil and vegetables and toss until cooked. Add the reserved duck meat and toss to warm through, and then add the oyster sauce.

TO SERVE: Spoon the roast duck mixture into the lettuce cups and garnish with the coriander sprigs. Serve with the consommé in a demitasse cup on the side and a small dish of fresh chilli.

MAKES 4 SERVINGS

Chilled Tomato Consommé,
Buffalo Mozzarella, Basil

TOMATO CONSOMMÉ

1kg (2lb 3oz) overripe tomatoes, preferably
    ox hearts
2 shallots, sliced
1 stick celery, chopped
dash of Worcestershire sauce
dash of Tabasco sauce
$^1/_4$tsp sea salt
$^1/_2$tsp sugar
30g (1oz) basil, roughly chopped

TO SERVE

4 balls buffalo mozzarella, each about
    100g (3$^1/_2$oz)
sea salt
juice of 1 lemon
50ml (1$^3/_4$fl oz) extra virgin olive oil
12 basil leaves
20ml ($^2/_3$oz) basil oil (see recipe, page 258)
24 slices black olive
20 croutons, 1 x 1cm ($^1/_2$ x $^1/_2$in), fried in butter

◆ This is the easiest consommé as it clarifies itself. Matched with the buffalo mozzarella and basil, it is a liquid version of the classic *insalata caprese*.

FOR THE TOMATO CONSOMMÉ: Chop the tomatoes roughly and place in a bowl with the shallots, celery, Worcestershire and Tabasco sauces. Season with the salt and a pinch of sugar. Cover and leave at room temperature for a couple of hours. Blend the contents of the bowl and place in a non-reactive saucepan. Bring the mixture to the boil and simmer for 10 minutes. Set up a chinoise sieve over a clean pot or bowl and line with muslin or an oil filter paper. Put the 30g (1oz) of basil leaves in the sieve, pour in the tomato 'stock' and leave to gently drip through the filter into the clean pan; do not press the solids through the sieve—the stock should be crystal clear. Chill well before use.

TO SERVE: Slice the mozzarella and season with sea salt, a squeeze of lemon juice and the extra virgin olive oil. Arrange the mozzarella in four shallow plates. Garnish with the olive slices, basil leaves and drops of basil oil. Pour the chilled tomato consommé over the garnish at the table and serve with the croutons.

MAKES 4 SERVINGS

Sweetcorn Veloute, Balmain Bug Dumplings

SWEETCORN VELOUTE

6 shallots, finely chopped

30g (1oz) butter

1tsp saffron powder

2 x 420g (15oz) tins sweetcorn kernels
    in brine

400ml (14fl oz) chicken stock

100ml (3^1/$_2$fl oz) cream

sea salt

juice of ^{1}/$_2$ lemon

BALMAIN BUG DUMPLINGS

4 balmain bugs

2tsp shallot confit (see recipe, page 264)

1tsp pickled ginger, julienned

12 gyoza or won ton wrappers

1 egg white

TO SERVE

40g (1^1/$_2$oz) butter

sea salt

juice of 1 lemon

micro coriander sprigs

◆ Sweetcorn is an ideal soup ingredient especially when married with seafood, as it is here with the bug meat dumplings. If you want to make the dish simpler, omit the dumplings and just add some flaked fresh crab meat. The best wine option would be a semillon or white bordeaux.

FOR THE SWEETCORN VELOUTE: In a saucepan, sweat the shallots in half the butter until soft but not coloured. Add the saffron powder and then all the sweetcorn, plus the brine from one tin. Bring to the boil and add the chicken stock. Simmer slowly for 30 minutes and then add the cream. Simmer for a few minutes more and liquidise the soup, then pass through a fine chinoise sieve. Correct seasoning with sea salt and a squeeze of lemon juice.

FOR THE BALMAIN BUG DUMPLINGS: Remove the bug meat from the shells and cut into large dice. Mix with the shallot confit and julienned ginger. Lay out the dumpling wrappers on a bench and brush with the egg white. Divide the bug mixture among the wrappers, then pull up the sides of each wrapper to make a small purse.

TO SERVE: Cook the dumplings in plenty of boiling salted water for about 2 minutes, until the dough is cooked. Remove with a slotted spoon and toss with the butter, season with sea salt and lemon juice. Arrange in four serving bowls and garnish with the coriander. Froth up the sweetcorn soup with a handheld blender. Put the soup into a jug and pour over the dumplings at the table.

MAKES 4 SERVINGS

Yabbie Bisque, Crushed Peas, Pecorino, Prosciutto, Basil, Mint

YABBIE BISQUE

200ml (7fl oz) champagne

6 shallots, sliced

1 baby fennel bulb, sliced

500g (17^1/$_2$oz) yabbies shells (or lobster
   or crab)

^{1}/$_2$tsp saffron powder

50ml (1^3/$_4$fl oz) Pernod

50ml (1^3/$_4$fl oz) cognac

100ml (3^1/$_2$fl oz) tomato passata

300ml (10^1/$_2$fl oz) chicken stock

200ml (7fl oz) cream

sea salt

juice of 1 lemon

CRUSHED PEAS

30g (1oz) butter

80g (2^1/$_2$oz) frozen peas

sea salt

20g (^{2}/$_3$oz) prosciutto trimmings, finely diced

20g (^{2}/$_3$oz) pecorino sardo, micro-planed

2tsp mixed chopped basil and mint

juice of 1 lemon

TO SERVE

16 yabbies, cooked (see method, page 65)

4 baby mint leaves

4Tbsp croutons fried in butter

50g (1^3/$_4$oz) crème fraiche

FOR THE YABBIE BISQUE: Put the champagne in a non-reactive saucepan with the shallots and fennel and reduce by three-quarters, then add the yabbie shells, saffron powder, Pernod and cognac. Using the tip of a rolling pin, crush the shells in the pan and then add the tomato passata and the stock. Simmer for 15 minutes and add the cream. Simmer for a further 15 minutes and then liquidise the soup, shells and all, in a blender and return to the stove. Cook slowly for another 15 minutes and then pass through a fine sieve or muslin cloth. Thin if needed with a little extra chicken stock. Correct the seasoning with sea salt and lemon juice. Keep warm.

FOR THE CRUSHED PEAS: Add the butter to a pan with the peas and heat up. Season with a little sea salt and crush with the back of a fork. Add the prosciutto and pecorino and then the chopped herbs. Correct the seasoning with a little sea salt and lemon juice.

TO SERVE: Warm the yabbies. Spoon some of the peas into four shallow bowls and arrange the yabbie tails on top with baby mint leaves. Sprinkle with the croutons and take to the table. Add the crème fraiche to the soup and blend with a handheld blender. Place the bisque in a jug and pour over the yabbies and peas at the table.

MAKES 4 SERVINGS

Potato, Leek and Truffle Soup

POTATO LEEK AND TRUFFLE SOUP

150g (1³/₄oz) white onions, finely sliced

250g (9oz) leeks, finely sliced

50g (1³/₄oz) butter

2 field or portobello mushrooms, sliced

20g (²/₃oz) truffle salsa or paste

200g (7oz) potatoes, peeled and evenly
   diced

700ml (24fl oz) white chicken stock, warmed

100ml (3¹/₂fl oz) cream

sea salt

juice of 1 lemon

TO SERVE

50g (1³/₄oz) crème fraiche or sour cream

as much fresh truffle as you can afford

2tsp chopped chives

FOR THE POTATO, LEEK AND TRUFFLE SOUP: Sweat the onions and leeks in the butter until soft but not coloured. Add the field mushrooms, truffle salsa and potatoes. Add the chicken stock and bring to the boil. Simmer slowly for about 30 minutes, until the potatoes are falling apart. Add the cream and simmer for a few minutes more and then puree the soup with a blender. Pass through a fine chinoise sieve. Correct the seasoning with sea salt and a squeeze of lemon juice.

TO SERVE: Froth up the soup with a handheld blender with the crème fraiche and pour into soup cups. Take to the table and grate the fresh truffle over the soup with a microplane. Sprinkle with chives.

MAKES 4 SERVINGS

POULTRY

& GAME BIRDS

On the care and training of waiters

Actors between jobs may act at being waiters, students play at being actors—and sometimes they are very good at it—but in the end there is no substitute for a professional waiter, a real one, the type who makes the care and service of the diners his or her life's purpose.

A 'real waiter' never walks to the kitchen empty handed or past his tables without scanning each to check whether anything is required or needs clearing away. The amateur may well get everything to the table without incident, but is rarely found scanning the other tables to see what needs doing next. The diner does not have to attract the attention of the real waiter—who is always there when needed—but the amateur often appears to be wearing blinkers.

A real waiter can store orders in her head and knows in an instant what all the guests have ordered and how far their meals have progressed. She remembers any special requests and idiosyncrasies from their last visit and keeps the chef informed. If a mistake happens in her 'section,' it is a calamity and not a giggle.

The real waiter will have started off laying tables and polishing cutlery. By the time he gets to converse with diners, he will know the menu and the chef's cooking style back to front—often better than new or junior kitchen members. Being able to describe each dish in an appetising way, without being condescending or superfluous, he advises diners and guides them through the menu so they have a balanced meal. A real waiter will be a fountain of reassurance, making his guests feel the chef is personally taking care of them.

ROAST PHEASANT BREAST

A real waiter gives service but is not servile. She is friendly but not over-familiar. She hears everything but comments on nothing. She is the epitome of diplomacy, treading a fine line between the diner's wants and expectations and the restaurant's ability to deliver.

Nothing fazes a real waiter and nothing is more exhilarating to him than a full house. Amateurs, on the other hand, get that 'rabbit caught in the headlights' look when faced with what essentially the restaurant has been designed for … being full!

Why are real waiters so few and far between down-under? Mainly because their occupation is still not considered a 'profession,' but simply a way for earning money. Of course, we do have some real waiters but we won't have a quorum of them until the job is taken seriously as a profession.

The history of the Inn—our first few weeks

The restaurant was finally open, better late than not at all, our first critic had eaten lunch and dinner and really most of things that could go wrong had. Or so we thought.

It was only five weeks until Christmas and then the summer break. Traditionally, these holidays are quiet for city restaurants but with the Inn being on the Hawkesbury we were hoping to get off to a busy start.

One of the most difficult things for any new restaurant is getting word out to the public that you are open and ready to wow them with your hospitality and culinary magic. This is where the restaurant review—for us, particularly one in the *Sydney Morning Herald*'s Good Living supplement—is worth its weight in gold, as long as it is favourable of course.

The first review is a double-edged sword. You need it for the sake of the business. But anyone who has anything to do with opening a new business, especially a restaurant, knows that, while you hit the ground running, it takes time for a restaurant to mature. It is like a great cheese or wine: early tastes give an indication of its promise but it takes time to show its full potential. We were concerned that we wouldn't receive our review until February as the *Herald* doesn't publish its supplement over Christmas and throughout January. But we weren't to be disappointed. The second weekend we were open, a booking for two turned out to be for the current *Sydney Morning Herald* reviewer and his predecessor. Of course, we were thrilled they were

in, but it was only our fifth service and we were still one staff member short on the floor and in the kitchen.

One of the most painful and stressful times in any chef's life is the interminable wait between the critic visiting the restaurant and the review being published. Ours was made worse because we were hoping for it to appear before the Christmas break rather than at the beginning of February. But, just as we wished, a couple of weeks later we had a favourable review, with a very respectable score of 17 out of 20. For a few short minutes we were relieved—it is always a gamble to take on what had once been a famous restaurant: not only are you being measured against your own standards but also against the place's history. Then the phones started ringing and within hours the restaurant was booked out for the following weekend.

With our first busy weekend looming, we arrived on Thursday morning and disaster struck. The motor on the punt, our workhorse delivery boat, packed up. A quick call to our boat mechanic and his even quicker verdict—it was 'stuffed', a technical term for it was never going to work at all, we needed a new one and it would take two or three weeks.

We still had the ferry and a tinnie, so we would have to make do. The restaurant was full and nothing was going to stop us.

The weekend progressed better than I hoped. Our systems held up well and the new menu concept, while producing a couple of small delays, worked reasonably well. Nothing that we couldn't fix with a bit of tinkering and practice.

We had a few more restaurant reviewers and food media through on the Saturday, as well as some faithful regulars from my other restaurant, Forty One, and excitement levels were still high on the Sunday morning. The guys were pumped and ready but, unfortunately, what wasn't pumped was the sewage system. Our first inkling of impending problems was shortly after service began and some unpleasant odours seemed to be arising from the pastry section. After the customary kitchen jokes about the pastry chef,

I thought it prudent to quickly check the source of the offensive smells.

Being in a remote location, we have a full grey-water sewage system that treats all effluent and kitchen waste. It appeared that after being reasonably dormant for a couple of years, the sudden onslaught of a full restaurant was causing issues. I had read in Gay Bilson's book *Plenty* that she'd had an ongoing love-hate relationship with the sewage system. Certainly Jeremy, our landlord, seemed to have an unnatural affection and enthusiasm for the system. But it was not an area I was keen to get down and dirty with, although it appeared the system had other ideas. So there I was, on our first full Sunday lunch, with a grease trap that was about to overflow and was producing some of the most disgusting smells I have had the displeasure of ingesting. A quick emergency call to Jeremy and we were lifting the lid of the tank. All we had to do was dislodge a float switch, which must have got stuck somewhere. Fifteen minutes later, the mission was accomplished and disaster averted. Thank goodness God invented

apprentices. The first battle with the 'sepo', as the staff would nickname our system, was won but the war would go on for quite a while yet.

The rest of the day passed without any more incidents and our third weekend—our first one full—had passed successfully. We cleaned down the restaurant. Spirits were high that Sunday evening as the sun started setting and a stunning red sky promised another beautiful day on the river.

All that was left to do was load up the boat with the dirty linen to be returned to the city and lock up. Then an ear-splitting scream pierced the peaceful night. One of the girls was dragging a full linen bag down the steps to the ferry when she came across a snake slithering slowly past the front door across the concrete, which still retained the sun's warmth from the balmy day.

I am a country boy at heart but in Switzerland we do not have deadly spiders, and snakes are as rare as hen's teeth. I have to admit I am not keen on either species. We all gathered at a safe distance from the reptile and discussed the best approach. It

did occur to me that any snake that was over a metre long with an ugly head and yellow stripes wasn't going to be particularly friendly.

Fortunately, on one side we have neighbours who have been on the river for a while and so we thought it prudent to gain some local advice. John was only to happy to help but, when he stood up from his comfortable chair, it became clear that maybe his courage was aided by the liberal amount of alcohol he had consumed that afternoon. Nevertheless, he was eager to get involved and anyone keen to get between me and a tiger snake is always welcome, inebriated or not.

We had actually planned for this eventuality—after all, we are located in the bush. Adrian was dispatched to the cellar to retrieve the snake-catching kit, a fancy name for a broom handle with a bag on the end of it. He returned empty-handed. Someone had moved the kit and no one knew where to.

John was unperturbed. Using a frame from a coffee plunger and a long stick, he managed to get the snake to curl itself around the plunger frame. Then, as he very carefully carried it, we loaded him and the snake onto the ferry and Adrian drove them across to the opposite bank where the snake was released.

On the drive home I reflected that operating a restaurant on a river in the middle of the Australian bush was going to offer many more challenges than those usually associated with restaurants. The fun was only just beginning.

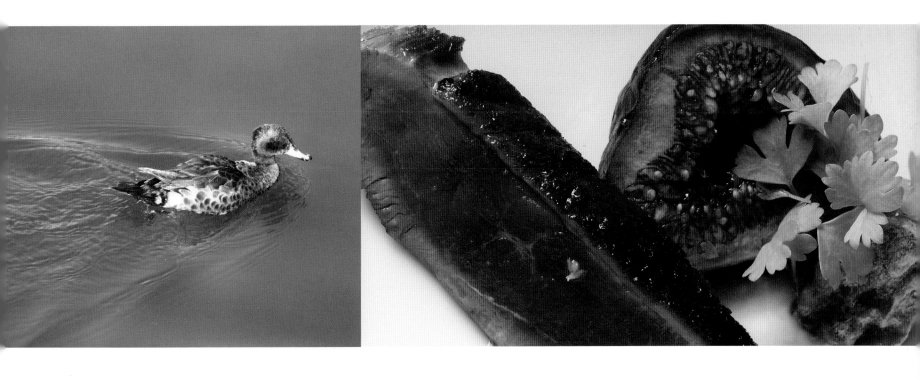

About the tools of the trade

From the very first time someone started cooking, back in the dark depths of history, they began using tools and equipment to assist them. We have come a long way from the first branch that was used to drag burned meat from a fire.

I am not that old, but when I started work as a young commis chef at the Savoy Hotel in London back in 1979 we were still cooking on coal-fired ranges. Granted, the hotel was probably the last place to convert to modern gas, but still it wasn't that far behind. In just the last 25 years the equipment and gadgets available to chefs has increased exponentially.

But still, with all these mod cons, most chefs list their favourite knife as their most valued piece of

kitchen equipment. I always find it amazing when I'm in someone's home kitchen and see that they do not possess any good knives. If there is one thing that is a good investment, it is a good knife or two.

Most of the standard kitchen equipment we know today was developed and refined by Alexis Soyer (1810–58), who perfected the field kitchens for the British army during the Crimean War and out of necessity designed the modern kitchen range. Much of this equipment didn't change radically for a century or so.

However, in the last decades there has been a rapid development in kitchen equipment. Some major changes, such as microwave ovens, have never really caught on in the professional kitchen.

While many home cooks seem to be happy to zap their dinner, most chefs have shunned the 'zap', no matter the convenience. It just doesn't seem acceptable. However, liquid nitrogen is another matter altogether!

Items like food processors, combi-steam ovens and induction cooking have all made life in the professional kitchen easier. As a young chef making a fish mousse, I had to mince the ingredients and then pass them through a fine sieve not once but up to eight times to attain the required result. With a food processor, a quick blitz and one easy pass through the tamis (drum) sieve and it is done.

Twenty years ago a food processor was a luxury, now it is standard equipment. Modern restaurant kitchens are now being equipped with nitrogen gas freeze-dryers, induction stoves, blast chillers, thermo baths and the like—and many of them look more like science laboratories.

With more technically advanced equipment, and the cooking techniques this enables, is the ability of the cook diminished? It is now possible to vacuum a rack of lamb, immerse it in a water bath in which the water is kept at a perfect 57°C and gently circulated, and after 40 minutes it is ready. The meat will cook through perfectly and evenly and not require a cook's skill to judge its doneness in the furnace of an unevenly heated oven. So it certainly does diminish the 'traditional' skills. On the other hand, you could also argue that mathematics is more complex today since the invention of the calculator and the computer; similarly, cooking will develop new skill sets based on the new cooking technologies. Still, it is handy to know long division for when there is a power cut and the computer is down.

With clever use of the technology available, the end product is better than that produced the old-fashioned way. So, apart from the nostalgia of days gone by, it is a lot easier being on the pass (the chef's term for inspecting dishes before they are sent out to diners) and getting exactly what you want served every time ... that is, if the cook has remembered to put the food on when the order came in!

Glenloth Squab Baked in Terracotta Clay, Winter Truffle Risotto

2 squabs

fresh winter truffles

20g (²/₃oz) butter, plus extra for serving

smoked sea salt

30ml (1fl oz) madeira

30g (1oz) garlic butter (see recipe, page 259)

greaseproof paper

1kg (2lb 3oz) soft red terracotta clay

WINTER TRUFFLE RISOTTO

20ml (²/₃oz) extra virgin olive oil

50g (1³/₄oz) shallots, finely chopped

250g (9oz) vialone nano rice

750ml (26¹/₂fl oz) good strong chicken stock
   (see recipe, page 260)

1tsp truffle salsa (see recipe, page 262)

40g (1¹/₂oz) cold butter, diced

30g (1oz) fontina cheese, grated

10g (¹/₃oz) fresh truffles

TO SERVE

120ml (4oz) truffle and madeira jus (see
   recipe, page 261)

a few leaves baby tat soi

◆ Squab is my favourite meat. The rich and tender dark red meat of the squab pigeon is plump and full of flavour. In this dish we pair the squab with the magical taste and aroma of winter truffles. To ensure the full aroma of the truffles is captured, the squab is cooked in terracotta clay (which you can buy at an art supply store). After baking, the squab encased in clay is taken to the table where the guest is invited to crack the clay open and release the heady aromas. The ideal wine to accompany this dish is a smooth burgundy from France or, if you are looking to the New World, then a Central Otago pinot noir.

FOR THE SQUABS: To prepare the squabs, remove the head and feet with a sharp knife and discard. Carefully remove the legs, being careful not to damage the skin on the breasts. Squab legs have little meat and can be used for stock. You will be left with the 'saddle' of squab. Insert a finger under the skin from the neck end of the bird and loosen without breaking it. Slice some of the truffles and season with smoked salt. Insert the slices carefully under the squab skin along the breast. Rub the squab with a little butter and quickly brown the 'saddle' in a hot pan, taking care not to cook the meat. Chill immediately.

   Preheat the oven to 250°C (475°F).

   When the squabs are cold, place each on a piece of silicon or baking paper approximately 30 x 30cm (12 x 12in). Season with a little more smoked salt, a splash of madeira and a knob of garlic butter. Pull up opposite sides of the paper to meet above the squab, fold in along the length, then fold over again lengthways; continue folding until the paper is flat against the squab saddle. Fold the ends of the paper under the squab and secure them in place with its weight. Roll out the terracotta clay between two sheets of silicone or baking paper until it is approximately 5mm (¼in) thick. Cut into two rectangles of

CONTINUES ON PAGE 148

30 x 45cm (12 x 18in). Place the squab parcel on the clay, breast side down, fold the clay up around the squab and turn over so the squab is the right way up and the clay is sealed underneath. Fold down the ends and crimp to close. Trim off the excess clay so you have a neat 'parcel'. Make a small hole in the top to allow the steam to escape while cooking. Repeat for the other three squabs. Place the squabs in the preheated oven for about 15 minutes.

FOR THE WINTER TRUFFLE RISOTTO: In a heavy-based pan, heat the olive oil and sweat off the shallot without colouring it. Add the rice and toast lightly, then add the hot stock and truffle salsa and stir well. Add 20g (²/₃oz) of the butter and stir to melt, cover the pan with the lid just off centre, and cook over a very low heat, checking every 5 minutes and stirring to prevent sticking. If at the last check the risotto is starting to look dry, then add some extra stock. After 20 minutes check the consistency of the rice to ensure it is cooked, add the grated fontina, the fresh truffle and the remaining butter and stir well. Cover the pan and leave off the heat for a couple of minutes before serving.

TO SERVE: Place the squabs in clay on a tray lined with fresh straw and take it to the table. Invite one of your guests to crack the clay with the back of a spoon and then open the silicone paper to release the wonderful aroma of the truffles and squab.

Take the squabs back to the kitchen and remove them from their wrappers. In a frying pan, roll the squabs in some hot butter to crisp the skin up and then de-bone the breasts. Spoon some of the risotto onto each plate and top with a squab breast. Spoon around some truffle and madeira jus and garnish with the baby tat soi leaves.

MAKES 4 SERVINGS

Seared Duck Breast, Grilled Balsamic Fig, Salted Walnuts, Foie Gras *Cromesquis*

2 duck breasts, skin on
250ml (9fl oz) poultry brine (see recipe,
    page 263)
GRILLED BALSAMIC FIGS
3 ripe figs
200ml (7fl oz) balsamic vinegar
100g (3^1/$_2$oz) sugar
2tsp mint leaves
CELERIAC PUREE
250ml (9fl oz) chicken stock
125ml (4^1/$_2$fl oz) cream
250g (9oz) celeriac, cut into 1cm (^{1}/$_2$in) dice
25g (^{3}/$_4$oz) butter
sea salt if needed
FOIE GRAS CROMESQUIS
150ml (5fl oz) port wine

75ml (2^1/$_2$fl oz) veal stock
100g (3^1/$_2$oz) foie gras *mi-cuit*
125ml (4^1/$_2$fl oz) cream
2^1/$_2$ gelatine leaves, titanium-strength
flour seasoned with sea salt and
    freshly ground white pepper
1 egg
grapeseed oil for deep-frying
100g (3^1/$_2$oz) fine white breadcrumbs
TO COMPLETE
1tsp chopped chives
a little butter for sautéeing
sea salt
12 salted walnuts (see recipe, page 258)
40ml (1^1/$_2$fl oz) green apple reduction
    (see recipe, page 75)

◆ We are unable to obtain fresh raw foie gras in Australia so I looked for a way to incorporate the *mi-cuit* (or half-cooked) foie gras that is available into a dish. The result was an adaptation of French three-star chef Michel Meneau's dish, foie gras *cromesquis*, a crisp breadcrumb cube that conceals a molten liquid foie gras. Naturally I combined this with duck breast and because figs were in season they were added to the dish. To cut the richness of the foie gras, the figs are marinated in balsamic.

Because of the acidity of the figs and the richness of the foie gras, this is a difficult dish to match wine to. Chateau D'Yquem would go beautifully with it, but for us lesser mortals a gewürztraminer or, if you prefer red wine, a pinot noir would be best.

FOR THE DUCK BREASTS: Lay the duck breasts on a board and lightly score the skin. Leave the duck breasts in a poultry brine for 2 hours. Remove from the brine and dry thoroughly. Place in individual vacuum pouches and seal on medium. Cook in a water bath at 60.5°C for 30 minutes.
FOR THE GRILLED BALSAMIC FIGS: Prick the whole figs all over with a pin. Heat a grill plate and lightly grill the figs to warm them through. Bring the balsamic vinegar to the boil with the sugar. Place

the warm grilled figs in a clip-top jar with the mint leaves and pour over the balsamic syrup. Marinate the figs for a least 24 hours.

FOR THE CELERIAC PUREE: Bring the chicken stock to the boil and reduce by half. Add the cream and bring back to the boil, then add the diced celeriac to the boiling liquid and cook for a few minutes until tender. Remove from the heat and strain off the liquid, reserving it. Place the hot celeriac in a blender, adding a little of the cooking liquor. Blend for a couple of minutes until you have a smooth puree. Put the puree back into a saucepan on the stove and whisk in the cold butter. Check seasoning and correct with sea salt if needed.

FOR THE FOIE GRAS CROMESQUIS: Reduce the port wine and the veal stock until you have about 100ml (3½fl oz) left, add the cream and crumbled gelatine leaves and warm up to 80°C (176°F). Pass the foie gras through a drum sieve, then slowly whisk it into the hot port-cream mixture and stir until smooth. Pour into a tray about 2cm (¾in) deep and set the mixture in the refrigerator.

When set, cut the foie gras mixture into 2cm cubes and freeze. When frozen, roll them in seasoned flour, egg wash and fine white breadcrumbs. Repeat the egg wash and breadcrumbs twice.

TO COMPLETE: Remove the duck from the vacuum pouch and place in a hot pan to crisp the skin. When nicely browned, remove from the pan and rest on a rack.

Deep-fry the *cromesquis* quickly at 200°C (400°F) until golden brown, then immediately remove them. Cut the top off the cube and sprinkle the molten foie gras with chopped chives.

Cut the grilled fig into quarters and sauté in a little butter.

Arrange a spoon of celeriac puree on each serving plate. Slice the duck lengthways, season each slice with sea salt and drape it across the puree with the foie gras to one side, a couple of salted walnuts, the balsamic fig quarters and finally a drizzle of green apple reduction.

MAKES 6 SERVINGS

Seared Duck Breast, Grilled Balsamic Fig, Salted Walnuts, Foie Gras *Cromesquis*

Roast Saltwater-soaked Quail, Morels and White Asparagus

6 large quails

500ml (17^1/$_2$oz) poultry brine (see recipe, page 263)

extra virgin olive oil

clarified butter for cooking

WHITE ASPARAGUS

12 large spears white asparagus, trimmings reserved

^{1}/$_2$tsp sugar

^{1}/$_2$tsp sea salt

70ml (2^1/$_4$fl oz) cold organic milk

MOREL MUSHROOMS

100g (3^1/$_2$oz) fresh morel mushrooms

75g (2^1/$_2$oz) butter

1tsp chopped garlic

50ml (1^3/$_4$fl oz) chicken stock

sea salt

ASPARAGUS AND MOREL VELOUTE SAUCE

75g (2^1/$_2$oz) dried morels, trimmings reserved

100ml (3^1/$_2$fl oz) madeira

50g (1^3/$_4$oz) shallots, sliced

1tsp butter

100g (3^1/$_2$oz) white asparagus trimmings (see above)

150ml (5fl oz) veal jus (see recipe, page 260)

300ml (10^1/$_2$fl oz) cream

sea salt

TO COMPLETE

butter

2tsp crème fraiche

◆ Earthy fresh morels and white asparagus have a lovely affinity. Here, the texture of the slow-cooked brined quail is a lovely counter to the crisp bite of the asparagus and the chewiness of the morels. This dish is best suited to a full-bodied chardonnay or light red such as a gamay.

FOR THE QUAIL: Remove the legs and wing tips from the quails, leaving the breasts on the bone as a 'saddle'. Soak the quail saddles for 1 hour in the poultry brine, then remove and dry well.

Place in individual vacuum pouches with a little extra virgin olive oil and seal on medium vacuum. Cook in a water bath at 57°C for 15 minutes. Remove from the water bath and pouch. Brown the 'saddles' in a little clarified butter. Rest for 5 minutes in a warm place and then de-bone the breasts.

FOR THE WHITE ASPARAGUS: Trim the tough ends off the asparagus, then peel and trim them all to the same length. Lay the asparagus spears in a single layer in a vacuum bag. Add the sugar and salt to milk and add to the vacuum bag. Seal on medium vacuum and place in a water bath at 85°C for about 45 minutes, until the asparagus feels tender to touch. Remove the pouch from the water bath and immerse in ice water to chill. Store in the vacuum bag until needed.

FOR THE MOREL MUSHROOMS: Trim the stems of the morels and reserve for the sauce. Soak the mushrooms in warm water—fresh morels trap dirt in their pores and warm water is the most effective

CONTINUES ON PAGE 156

way of cleaning them. Change the water a couple of times and then drain the morels on an absorbent paper towel.

Trim the morels: if large split them, if small leave them whole. Keep any trimmings for the sauce. Melt the butter in a frying pan, add the garlic and sweat without colouring. Add the morels, toss in the butter and garlic, and then add the chicken stock. Place a lid on the pan and stew the morels for a few minutes until they are tender. Drain and season lightly with sea salt.

FOR THE ASPARAGUS AND MOREL VELOUTE SAUCE: Soak the dried morels in the madeira for 1 hour. In a saucepan sweat the shallots in the butter, add the white asparagus and morel trimmings, then the dried morels and madeira. Reduce until the madeira has almost evaporated and then add the veal jus, bring to the boil and add the cream. Simmer gently on a low heat until the sauce coats the back of a spoon.

Remove from the heat and place the mixture in a blender and give it a quick blitz. Pass through a fine chinois sieve lined with muslin, then pass a second time to ensure the sauce is velvety. Season to taste with sea salt if necessary.

TO COMPLETE: Remove the asparagus from the vacuum bag and discard the milk. Cut each asparagus spear into three even lengths and toss in a little butter heated in a saucepan, then add the fresh morels. Arrange the asparagus and morels on each serving plate. Place two quail breasts on each pile of asparagus. Place the warm sauce in a jug and, using a handheld blender, froth the crème fraiche into the sauce. Spoon a little froth and sauce over the quail.

MAKES 6 SERVINGS

Roast Pheasant Breast, Asparagus Duxelle, Oysters and Caviar

2 pheasant breasts
300ml (10¹/₂fl oz) poultry brine (see recipe,
    page 263)

ASPARAGUS DUXELLE

1 bunch green asparagus
6 small shallots, peeled
20g (²/₃oz) butter
sea salt

CAVIAR AND OYSTER VELOUTE

8 pacific oysters in their shells

200ml (7fl oz) champagne veloute
    (see recipe, page 261)
15g (¹/₂oz) crème fraiche
1tsp lemon juice

TO COMPLETE

150ml (5fl oz) cooking sake
butter for cooking
sea salt and freshly ground white pepper
25g (³/₄oz) oscietra caviar
1tsp chives, finely chopped

◆   I am extending the marriage of the sea and the land with the addition of briny caviar. Australian pheasants have a much milder, less gamey flavour than their European cousins and benefit from the extra dimension the oysters and caviar bring. I would drink a chablis or dry riesling with it—or even a gavi.

FOR THE THE PHEASANT: Place the pheasant breasts in the poultry brine. Marinate for 1½ hours, then remove from brine and dry. Place in individual vacuum pouches with a sprig of lemon thyme and seal. Poach in a water bath at 60.5°C for 30 minutes.

FOR THE ASPARAGUS DUXELLE: If using large asparagus, peel them from just under the tip. Cut the top 4cm (1½in) off the asparagus and reserve these tips. Using a sharp knife, cut the asparagus stalks and then the shallots into fine dice. Melt the butter in a pan and sweat the shallots without colouring. Add the finely diced asparagus and sweat gently until cooked without colouring. Season to taste.

FOR THE CAVIAR AND OYSTER VELOUTE: Open the oysters carefully over a small bowl and capture the oyster juices. Bring the veloute to the boil and then remove from the stove. Pour into a stainless steel jug and add the oyster juice, crème fraiche and lemon juice. Blitz with a blender and keep warm.

TO COMPLETE: Heat the sake to 45°C (113°F) and add the oysters to warm through. Remove the pheasant from the pouches and crisp the skins in the butter in a hot frying pan. Remove from pan and rest for a few minutes. Cook the asparagus tips in boiling salted water; drain and toss with a little butter and seasoning. Spoon some of the asparagus duxelle into the reserved oyster shells and place a drained oyster on top. Arrange on serving plates. Carve each pheasant breast into slices and arrange on the plates with the asparagus tips. To make the sauce, blitz the oyster veloute with a handheld blender and then gently stir through the caviar and chives. Drizzle the sauce over the pheasant and oysters on the plate.

MAKES 4 SERVINGS

Roast Organic Chicken, the Old-fashioned Way

THE CHICKEN

1 organic chicken, about 1.5kg (3lb 4^1/$_2$oz)

100ml (3^1/$_2$fl oz) extra virgin olive oil

smoked sea salt

2 sprigs rosemary

THE VEGETABLES

12 shallots, peeled

sea salt

150ml (5fl oz) olive oil

100g (3^1/$_2$oz) garlic butter

12 baby carrots, peeled

1 butternut pumpkin, cut into slices

3 leeks

TO COMPLETE

100g (3^1/$_2$oz) butter

juice of 1 lemon

30g (1 oz) parsley, roughly chopped

15g (^{1}/$_2$oz) tarragon, roughly chopped

◆   There is nothing more satisfying than a simple roast chicken. It is more of a home dish than a restaurant one but is still the best way to eat chicken. Serve it with a mesclun salad tossed in aged balsamic and extra virgin olive oil and a side dish of spaetzli noodles (see recipe, page 86). Enjoy it with a bottle of pinot noir or a nice merlot.

FOR THE CHICKEN: Preheat the oven to 200°C (400°F). Wash and dry the chicken. Place it on a wire rack in a deep roasting tray and sprinkle with the extra virgin olive oil and smoked sea salt. Place the rosemary sprigs in the cavity of the chicken. Pour some boiling water into the roasting tray under the rack—the water gently steams the chicken while it is roasting and keeps it moist.

Roast the chicken in the hot oven for 20 minutes, then turn the heat down to 175°C (345°F) for a further 40–50 minutes, depending on the size of the chicken.

FOR THE VEGETABLES: Roll out a sheet of aluminium foil and place the shallots on it. Season well with sea salt, drizzle with olive oil and put a small knob of garlic butter on top. Seal the shallots in the foil. Repeat the process for the baby carrots, the pumpkin and the leeks. Place the parcels of carrots, pumpkin and leeks on a tray in the bottom of the oven and cook for 30–40 minutes, until tender. Add the carrots a little later—they will take about 20 minutes.

TO COMPLETE: Remove the chicken from the oven and rest it for 10 minutes. Arrange the vegetables on a platter. Carve the chicken and arrange the pieces on the vegetables.

Put the remaining butter in a hot frying pan and cook until it foams and sizzles and starts to go a golden colour, add the lemon juice, then remove from the heat and add the herbs. Pour the sauce over the chicken.

MAKES 4 SERVINGS

BUTCHER'S MEAT

On brining

In cooking, brining is a process similar to marinating: the meat or fish is soaked before cooking. Brining hydrates the cells of the muscle tissue, making the meat moister.

When you make a salt-and-water solution and add a piece of meat or fish, a scientific process called osmosis begins. This process seeks to equalise the amount of salt on the outside of the flesh with the amount on the inside. It is an extremely simple process. The major danger is that over-brining not only results in an over-salted product but also changes the texture of the meat or fish.

Because there is little, if any, salt inside most raw meats, the salt and water is drawn deep into the meat fibres. The great thing about this process is that you can add spices, herbs and other flavourings to the salt-water solution and it will get drawn into the meat tissues as well. This adds layers of subtle flavours to meats and fish by infusion rather than by seasoning on the surface.

It is a good idea to make the brine the day before and ensure it is chilled before adding the meat or fish, which should never be put into a warm or hot brine. Experimentation will determine the length of time that you brine the meat and fish. See Basic Recipes, page 256, for meat and poultry brines.

Thoughts about the restaurant reviewer

Everyone has particular skills, some more obvious than others. Most people know if they are good dancers, singers or mathematicians or whether they are not. Strangely, everyone believes they are skilled tasters and eaters. Yet taste, like other faculties, must be learned and developed through practice. I can belt out a tune but by no stretch of the imagination am I a singer that anyone in their right mind would want to listen to. But suggest to someone that they do not have an educated food palate and they will look at you

as if you are an idiot. Oddly enough, if you suggest their wine palate is not up to scratch, most people agree with you—mainly because of the pretension and pomposity that often accompanies fine wines. I often think that if I harped on about 'comestibles' as the wine experts go on about fermented grape juice, everyone would think I was a complete wanker … However, I digress. The fact is expert tasters dedicate years to training their palates, whatever their field.

To learn anything well is to discover over and over how little you really know. Everyone is a food critic: every time any one of us places something in our mouth we make a judgement about whether or not we like it. Does this make everyone an expert? Well, it makes them an expert on what they do

or don't like but not an expert on the subject of food tastes.

For thousands of years, humans have been discussing food—after all, if it is worth eating then it is worth discussing. From Apicius to Brillat-Savarin to our modern-day scribes, not only has food been described and argued about, but it has been the source of inspiration for billions of written pages and of course blogs and twitters as well. It is interesting that along with the advent of the celebrity chef, we have seen the growth of an entire industry of food journalism. It is a symbiotic relationship of love and hate but, in the final analysis, both sides need each other.

As a chef and restaurateur, I applaud the skilled palates, journalistic talent and visionary insight of those critics who have raved about my restaurants

and been kind to us over the years … of course, those reviews that have been less favourable were obviously written by foodie charlatans who have their tastebuds located in the nether regions and are a disgrace to their pathetic parasitic excuse for a profession. These are sentiments shared by all chefs and restaurateurs. A good review is essential to the success of a restaurant. It will bring customers through the door, although it is then up to the restaurant to be good enough to keep those diners coming back.

Restaurant reviews and guidebooks are an important part of our industry these days. What the Michelin brothers started in 1904 as a guide for chauffeurs of the new-fangled invention, the motor car, has blossomed into a worldwide industry. The original *Guide Michelin* was a list of establishments

that put on a 'good table', directing wealthy travellers to reputable restaurants for their daily repast. Today the *Michelin* is still the most respected and coveted guide in the world and, despite its critics, is the one that chefs hold in most awe and respect.

Restaurant guides and reviews take many forms, from the sparse prose and symbols of the *Guide Michelin* to the ramblings of such writers as AA Gill, who spend most of their reviews talking about some inane subject that very often only has a tenuous link to the actual restaurant under review. I have to admit, though, Mr Gill has an addictive style and I love reading his reviews, especially as I'm fairly secure in the knowledge that he and the London *Times* will not be reviewing in the Hawkesbury River region anytime soon.

In his very early years, Terry Durack wrote one

of the best reviews I have ever read, of the Auberge d'Illhausern in Alsace, which has three Michelin stars. The Auberge sits on the beautiful shores of the river Ill and was originally a simple local restaurant, exactly like the one on the riverbank directly opposite. It went on to become a world-famous temple of gastronomy, while the restaurant across the river maintained its peasant roots and kept serving the local fare. In an entertaining, humorous review, Terry compared the two restaurants—and each in its own way came out as a winner. It was what a good review should be: entertaining, informative, humorous and educational. A few years later, when we were passing through Alsace, we headed not to the Auberge, where I had dined before, but to the local haunt across the river.

By its very nature, a review can never be taken as a general comment because it is always a subjective reaction to a particular person's experiences on one or more occasions—a personal experience that might not even be shared by someone else dining at the same table on the same evening. In the ideal world, a restaurant would be visited by a multitude of reviewers over many visits to gauge its consistency. Expert food tasters with an encyclopaedic knowledge of culinary practices and ingredients would do all this anonymously. They would know their culinary history and get all their facts correct, they would not praise chefs for creativity when the chef in question is just plagiarising another's creations. These critics would bear in mind the philosophy of the restaurant and what the chef is trying to achieve—not what the critic thinks it should be. They would put aside their preconceived ideas of the restaurant and of the chef and judge their evening as a complete experience from the point of view of the types of diners that the restaurant is aimed at. They would then write a witty and educational piece that perfectly sums up what a new diner is likely to experience upon taking their recommendation, and then allocate a rating that is fair within a system that takes into account the various styles and levels of restaurants, their value for money, quality level and target audience. Quite simple really.

My view of food critics over the years has changed little. I assume that by and large they are a decent group of people trying to earn a living, like the rest of us. Mostly, they have enjoyed what I have done in my restaurants and given me support—and for that I am grateful. Over the years a couple of critics have not understood what we are doing or, just through bad luck, hit the restaurant on a bad day—and every restaurant has bad days. In the end, we have to accept the good with the bad and try harder next time. But it is important that diners recognise a review for what it is: one person's opinion. Chefs and restaurateurs should also accept reviews for what they might reflect—a discrepancy between what they are trying to accomplish and what the critic perceived. Most often, when people disagree with a review, they are expressing a difference in taste. And differences in taste are virtually impossible to resolve.

I have an insatiable appetite for knowledge when it comes to all things related to the restaurant world and I have always wanted to dine out with a leading food critic who is reviewing to get to know what they are actually thinking. Now, that would be an interesting and insightful discussion.

BRAISED OX CHEEK AND GRILLED SIRLOIN STEAK

Wagyu 'Minute Steak', Native Pepper Paste, Caramelised Onions, Jerusalem Artichokes

2 white onions, sliced

3Tbsp butter

sea salt

JERUSALEM ARTICHOKE FONDANTS

100g (3^1/$_2$oz) butter

12 large Jerusalem artichokes, peeled
    and trimmed

2 sprigs lemon thyme

sea salt

100ml (3^1/$_2$fl oz) chicken stock

THE MINUTE STEAK

4 x 100g (3^1/$_2$oz) wagyu sirloin minute steaks

20g (^{2}/$_3$oz) native pepper paste (see recipe,
    page 258)

50g (1^3/$_4$oz) butter

TO COMPLETE

80ml (2^1/$_2$fl oz) veal jus (see recipe, page 260)

100g (3^1/$_2$oz) Jerusalem artichoke puree (see
    recipe, page 264)

chopped chives

micro parsley

FOR THE CARAMELISED ONIONS: Heat the onions and butter with some sea salt in a heavy-based saucepan and gently sweat until the onions are soft. Turn up the heat and keep stirring while the onions caramelise and go a golden brown.

FOR THE JERUSALEM ARTICHOKE FONDANTS: In a heavy-based saucepan, heat the butter and add the trimmed Jerusalem artichokes and the lemon thyme. Season with sea salt and cook over low heat until the artichokes start to colour, then add the stock and cover. Cook slowly until the stock and butter have almost evaporated and the artichokes are golden and soft.

FOR THE MINUTE STEAK: Brush the steaks with the pepper paste and sear in a hot, heavy-based frying pan for 45 seconds on each side. Remove from the pan and top with the caramelised onions.

TO COMPLETE: Heat the veal jus. Heat the artichoke puree and then spoon some onto the serving plates. Arrange the minute steak on top, place the artichoke fondants next to the steak and drizzle some veal jus around. Sprinkle with chopped chives and micro parsley.

MAKES 4 SERVINGS

Organic Pork Belly, Lemon-braised Mud Crab, Gratinated Pumpkin Puree

320g (11oz) organic pork belly

500ml (17¹/₂oz) meat brine (see recipe,
    page 263)

2 sprigs lemon thyme

100g (3¹/₂oz) sea salt

250g (9oz) butternut pumpkin, peeled
    and diced

3 shallots, finely sliced

50g (1³/₄oz) kassler bacon, finely sliced

1 clove garlic, crushed

100ml (3¹/₂fl oz) extra virgin olive oil

sea salt

80g (2¹/₂oz) fontina cheese, grated

50g (1³/₄oz) unsalted butter

50ml (1³/₄fl oz) champagne veloute (see
    recipe, page 261)

juice of 1 lemon

200g (7oz) mud crab meat, handpicked

1tsp pickled lemon rind, finely diced

sea salt if needed

8 gyoza wrappers

1 egg white

sea salt

lemon juice

2 knobs of butter

80ml (2¹/₂fl oz) crustacean veloute (see recipe,
    page 261)

micro coriander

◆ Pork belly is rich and unctuous. Coupled with silky lemon and mud crab dumplings, this is one of my favourite ways to enjoy pork. Open a bottle of sancerre or New World sauvignon blanc to cut through the richness of the dish.

FOR THE PORK BELLY: Trim the pork belly into a neat rectangle and set in the brine for 3 hours. Remove from the brine and rinse. Dry the pork thoroughly and place in a vacuum pouch with the lemon thyme. Seal on high and poach the pork belly in a water bath at 84°C for 8 hours. When the meat feels tender, place the vacuum pouch in an ice-water bath to chill, then remove and press under a light weight overnight.

FOR THE PUMPKIN: Preheat the oven to 180°C (350°F). In a bowl, toss the pumpkin with the shallots, bacon, garlic and olive oil; season with sea salt. Spread out a sheet of aluminium foil and pile the pumpkin mixture onto it. Seal the foil around the pumpkin and place on a tray in the heated oven for 30 minutes, until the pumpkin is tender.

Remove from the oven, open the foil and sprinkle the cheese over the pumpkin. Return the open parcel to the oven for a few minutes to melt the cheese. Mix in the butter, then blend the

pumpkin to a smooth puree. Correct the seasoning with sea salt. Turn the oven up to 200°C (400°F).

FOR THE CRAB MEAT: Heat the veloute, add the lemon juice and then reduce by half. Cool and mix the liquid through the crab meat, with the pickled lemon rind. Taste for seasoning and adjust with a little sea salt if needed. Lay the gyoza wrappers out on a bench and brush with egg white. Spoon some crab meat onto each wrapper and seal like a beggar's purse.

TO COMPLETE: Remove the pork belly from the vacuum pack and wipe off any gel. Score the skin side with a sharp knife and rub the top with sea salt. Place the pork, salted skin side down, in a heavy-based ovenproof pan and place over medium heat; once it starts crisping, place the pan in the 200°C (400°F) oven to finish heating the pork belly through. Slice the meat.

Poach the crab dumplings in plenty of boiling salted water, drain and toss with a squeeze of lemon and some butter.

Reheat the pumpkin puree with a small knob of butter.

Spoon some puree onto the serving plates and arrange the sliced pork belly and crab dumplings. Heat the shellfish veloute and then foam up with a handheld blender; spoon some over the dumplings and garnish with micro coriander.

MAKES 4 SERVINGS

Organic Pork Belly, Lemon-braised Mud Crab, Gratinated Pumpkin Puree

Lamb Shank, Bone Marrow Dumpling, Baby Spinach, Olive Jus

Lamb Shank, Bone Marrow Dumpling, Baby Spinach, Olive Jus

THE LAMB SHANKS

100g (3½oz) large black kalamata olives

2 lamb shanks, hind

8 shallots, sliced

1 clove garlic

300ml (10½fl oz) madeira

20g (⅔oz) dried porcini mushrooms

300ml (10½fl oz) chicken stock

sea salt

80g (2½oz) caramelised onions (see
    recipe, page 171)

8 large spinach leaves

BONE MARROW DUMPLING

80g (2½oz) bone marrow, soaked and
    cleaned

150g (5oz) fresh white breadcrumbs

½tsp sea salt

½tsp lemon thyme leaves

1tsp chopped flatleaf parsley

1 organic egg (60g/2oz)

60ml (2fl oz) cream

TO COMPLETE

smoked sea salt

200g (7oz) baby spinach leaves

butter

sea salt

8 roast shallots (see recipe, page 264)

80ml (2½fl oz) 'French onion soup' puree
    (see recipe, page 107)

1 tomato, peeled, seeded and diced

◆ Lamb shanks are a great winter dish but a little too rustic for a degustation menu, so I remove the meat, wrap it in a bone marrow dumpling dough and steam it. The result is so popular that I have to include the dish on the menu every winter. Match it with a merlot or cabernet blend.

FOR THE BRAISED LAMB SHANKS: Pit the olives, reserving the stones, and finely dice the olive flesh; set aside. Season the lamb shanks and sear in a heated, heavy-based pan until they have a good colour all around. Remove from the pan and set aside. Add the shallots and garlic to the pan and fry until golden, then add the madeira and porcini and cook until the liquid has reduced by three-quarters. Add the stock and olive stones and reduce the liquid by half again. Strain off the stock through a fine chinoise sieve. Return the stock to the stove and reduce by half, whisk in a knob of butter and pass through a muslin cloth.

Place the lamb shank in a vacuum pouch and add the stock. Seal the bag and cook in a water bath at 85°C for 8 hours. Remove the lamb shanks from the bag, reserving the cooking liquid. Take the meat off the bone. Place two rectangles of clingfilm on the bench and lay out the meat on the film. Season with sea salt and cover with the caramelised onions. Roll up to form two sausages, each about 3cm (1¼in) in diameter.

Blanch the spinach leaves in boiling water and then plunge them into an ice bath. Remove the spinach and dry. Lay four of the spinach leaves, overlapping them, on a piece of clingfilm to form

a rectangle. Remove one of the lamb shank 'sausages' from its wrapping and place on the spinach leaves, then roll up tightly to make a fatter 'sausage'. Repeat with the remaining spinach and lamb shank. Chill for a couple of hours in the refrigerator.

FOR THE BONE MARROW DOUGH: Pass the bone marrow through a drum sieve to get rid of any sinew and place in a food mixer. Blitz quickly for 15 seconds and then add the other ingredients. Mix on full speed for 10 seconds—do not overmix the dough. Wrap the dough in clingfilm and chill for 1 hour.

Remove the dough from the refrigerator and slice in two lengthways. Place a piece of dough between two sheets of silicone or baking paper and roll out to about 5mm (¼in) thickness. Unwrap the clingfilm from a spinach-covered lamb shank, place on the dough, roll up and trim the edges. Repeat with the remaining dough and shank. Rewrap each in clingfilm, tying off each end, then wrap tightly in aluminium foil. Poach the dumplings in a water bath at 82°C for 40 minutes.

TO COMPLETE: Unwrap the dumplings and cut in half crossways. Season with a little smoked sea salt. Warm the shallots in the oven or a frying pan, and gently reheat the onion puree in a saucepan. Wilt the baby spinach in a little butter and season with sea salt. Arrange on the serving plates with the roasted shallots and a smear of the onion puree. Place the half-dumpling on the puree. Add the tomato and olive dice to the stock, reheat and spoon over the shank.

MAKES 4 SERVINGS

Braised Ox Cheek and Grilled Sirloin, Wild Mushrooms, Pommes Puree

BRAISED OX CHEEK

1 wagyu ox cheek, about 400g (14oz)

8 shallots, sliced

1 clove garlic

300ml (10^1/$_2$fl oz) madeira

20g (^{2}/$_3$oz) dried porcini mushrooms

300ml (10^1/$_2$fl oz) chicken stock

1tsp butter

THE SIRLOIN

300g (10oz) wagyu sirloin steak, marble
score 9+, trimmed

100ml (3^1/$_2$fl oz) garlic oil

20g (^{2}/$_3$oz) garlic butter (see recipe, page 259)

1tsp smoked sea salt

THE MUSHROOMS

200g (7oz) mixed wild mushrooms, cleaned

100g (3^1/$_2$oz) butter

sea salt

50g (1^3/$_4$oz) shallot confit, finely diced (see
recipe, page 264)

100ml (3^1/$_2$fl oz) chicken stock

TO COMPLETE

100g (3^1/$_2$oz) pommes puree (see recipe,
page 264)

8 roast shallots (see recipe, page 264)

12 sprigs chervil

◆ I always enjoy contrasts, whether between meat and seafood or different cuts of the same animal.

FOR THE BRAISED OX CHEEK: Season the ox cheeks and place in a heated pan. Sear until they have a good colour all around. Remove from the pan; add the shallots and garlic and fry until golden. Add the madeira and dried porcini and cook until the liquid has reduced by three-quarters. Add the stock and reduce by half again, then strain off through a fine chinoise sieve and reserve. Place the ox cheek in a vacuum bag, add the stock and seal. Cook in a water bath at 83°C for 8 hours until tender to touch. Plunge the bag into an ice bath. When cold, remove the meat from the bag, reserving the cooking liquid. Re-vacuum the meat in a new bag. Heat the cooking liquid over medium and reduce by half. Whisk in the butter and keep warm.

FOR THE SIRLOIN: Seal the sirloin in a vacuum pouch with the garlic oil. Cook in a water bath at 85°C for 20 minutes. Remove the meat from the pouch and quickly char on a hot grill on each side. Brush with the garlic butter and season with smoked sea salt. Rest in a warm place for 15 minutes.

FOR THE MUSHROOMS: Heat the butter in the pan with the mushrooms and season with sea salt. As the butter melts, toss the mushrooms to coat with the butter. Add the shallots and chicken stock, cook until the stock has evaporated, tossing the mushrooms all the time. Taste and season with sea salt.

TO COMPLETE: Place the ox cheek bag in a water bath at 95°C to reheat. Heat the pommes puree. Arrange the sliced sirlion and ox cheek on the puree on serving plates, sprinkle with the mushrooms and shallots. Pour the sauce around and garnish with sprigs of chervil.

MAKES 4 SERVINGS

Roast Gippsland Lamb Rack, Sweet Green Peas, Wilted Lettuce, Lemon Myrtle

THE LAMB RACK

1 lamb rack, trimmed and frenched

1 sprig lemon thyme

1 sprig rosemary

50ml (1³/₄fl oz) garlic oil

THE PEAS

200g (7oz) frozen baby green peas

20ml (²/₃oz) extra virgin olive oil

50g (1³/₄oz) butter

50ml (1³/₄fl oz) cream

THE SAUCE

20ml (²/₃oz) champagne

1tsp powdered lemon myrtle

100ml (3¹/₂fl oz) champagne veloute (see recipe page, 261)

²/₃tsp soy lecithin

TO COMPLETE

1 head baby cos lettuce

50g (1³/₄oz) butter

4 pommes anna (see recipe, page 265)

◆ I was introduced to Castricum lamb from Victoria by Peter Knipp, a good friend and then executive chef at Raffles Hotel in Singapore. Peter was singing the praises of his lamb from Australia and after a taste test I was convinced. On returning down-under, I got my butcher to source the lamb for Forty One Restaurant and have been using this excellent product ever since. The dish is best suited to a merlot.

FOR THE LAMB RACK: Place the lamb rack in a vacuum pouch with the herbs and garlic oil and seal on high. Poach in a water bath at 62°C for 50 minutes. Remove from the vacuum bag and discard the herbs. Sear the lamb rack in a heavy-based pan and rest in a warm place for 20 minutes.

FOR THE PEAS: Place the peas in a pan with the olive oil, butter and cream. Season with sea salt. Cook until the peas are soft, about 5 minutes, and then drain into a colander. Puree the peas in a blender on high for 2 minutes. Chill the puree over ice if not using straight away. To reheat, place in a pan with a small knob of butter and stir until hot; correct seasoning with sea salt.

FOR THE SAUCE: Put the champagne in a non-reactive pan and heat with the powdered lemon myrtle. When it comes to the boil, add the veloute and simmer for 5 minutes. Remove from the heat and leave to infuse for 20 minutes. Strain through a fine chinoise sieve and reheat. Add a squeeze of lemon juice and the soy lecithin and blitz with a handheld blender to foam.

TO COMPLETE: Cut the baby cos into quarters and wilt in the butter over high heat. Season with sea salt and arrange on serving plates with the pea puree, a slice of the lamb rack and the foamed sauce. Serve with pommes anna on the side.

MAKES 4 SERVINGS

Poached Veal Fillet, Langoustine, Leeks, Caviar Veloute

THE VEAL

320g (11oz) white milk-fed veal fillet or loin

20ml (²/₃fl oz) garlic oil

1 sprig lemon thyme

THE LANGOUSTINE

4 large langoustines or scampi

1 large leek

20g (²/₃oz) butter

pinch of smoked sea salt

juice of 1 lemon

TO COMPLETE

12 pencil leeks

20g (²/₃oz) oscietra caviar

80ml (2¹/₂fl oz) champagne veloute (see
   recipe, page 261)

12 sprigs chervil

◆ It is very hard to find good quality white, milk-fed veal in Australia but once in a while a producer gets it right. The delicate nature of milk-fed veal lends itself to matching the langoustines, and the caviar is the ideal 'seasoning'. A chardonnay or a shot of vodka goes nicely with this.

FOR THE VEAL: Place the veal fillet in a vacuum pouch with the garlic oil and lemon thyme and seal on high. Poach in a water bath at 62°C for 50 minutes. Remove the meat from the vacuum bag and discard the herbs. Rest the veal in a warm place for 20 minutes.

FOR THE LANGOUSTINE: Peel the langoustines, leaving on the tail fans and reserving the shells for a soup or crustacean veloute (see recipe, page 261).

Cut the leek crossways for a 10cm (4in) section of the whole leek, then slice that carefully down its length but only halfway through—take off the 4 outer layers, making 4 large rectangles of leek. Blanch these rectangles in boiling salted water and refresh in ice water. Drain and dry on a towel.

Turn the langoustine over so the underside is up. Using a sharp knife, make a small nick in a couple of places along its back to stop it from curling up when cooking.

Lay out the 4 rectangles of leek and carefully roll up a langoustine in each. Brush the top with softened butter and chill before cooking.

To cook, heat a non-stick pan. When hot, place the langoustine, butter side down, in the pan and cook for a minute until browned, and then turn over and finish cooking for a further minute. Squeeze with lemon juice and season with smoked sea salt.

TO COMPLETE: Cook the baby pencil leeks in plenty of salted boiling water. Drain, season and toss in a little knob of butter. For the sauce, heat the champagne veloute and add the caviar.

Slice the veal and arrange the medallions on serving plates next to the sautéed langoustine. Arrange the baby leeks by the veal and spoon the sauce generously around. Garnish with the sprigs of chervil.

MAKES 4 SERVINGS

GAME

MEAT & OFFAL

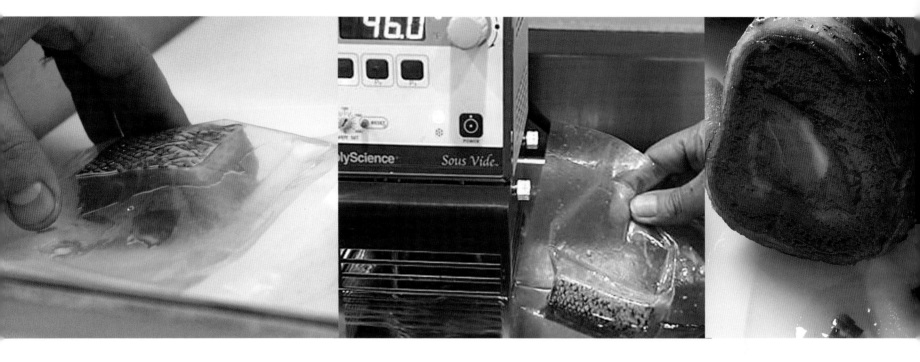

On *sous-vide*

In the early 1980s I was fascinated that the Roux brothers in London were experimenting with *sous-vide*, the original cook-chill system. They were mainly using it to store and reheat cooked food. Later that decade, when I was working in Hong Kong, I had my first access to a vacuum-packing machine. I started experimenting but was unhappy with the results of using cooked foods in the *sous-vide*. I quickly worked out that vacuuming raw food and then cooking in the *sous-vide* bag for à la carte cooking gave lovely results and much greater control. Many chefs have discovered this for themselves, but it has taken until now for the technique to become widely publicised.

At our restaurants we use this method extensively because, if the procedure is followed correctly, the results are perfect every time. With *sous-vide* we can cook precisely and it allows us to prepare some dishes that could not be made with conventional cooking methods, such as braising a short rib and maintaining a rare texture while rendering the meat perfectly tender. The method lends itself to cooking meat, fish, fruit and vegetables. Even some sauces and stocks are best prepared *sous-vide*.

Cooking in a bain marie, or water bath, is not new and is part of the classical repertoire. But today it is far more sophisticated. We checked the water temperature in the early days by sticking our hand in the water bath. Now the immersion circulator, used with the vacuum-packing machine, has changed the professional kitchen. The vacuum packer removes

oxygen from the pouch, compresses the food and seals the bag—at the compression strength you want (in recipes in this book, food is compressed at the normal setting unless specified). The immersion circulator is a device that is a combination thermometer, heater and pump that monitors and maintains the water at the temperature you set it to. And it moves the water around so that the temperature is even throughout the water bath. It means we can now seal the food tightly in a vacuum pouch and cook it at a low temperature in a way that excludes any outside interference or loss of juices. With experimentation, these two tools have opened a whole world of creativity. Now *sous-vide* water baths, circulators and vacuum packers are must-have equipment in all serious restaurant kitchens.

Several domestic models are now available for the home cook.

Sous-vide is not a complicated or mysterious system but rather a simple way to achieve consistency and also to prepare food in new and interesting ways. The most obvious benefit of being able to cook at controlled low temperatures is that it ensures against under- or over-cooking. But it also concentrates the flavours—because none are lost during the cooking process. Braising is one method of cooking that is transformed by the *sous-vide* method. In traditional braising you are cooking at temperatures in excess of 85°C (temperatures are always in Celsius). However, at around 69°C the meat you are braising loses most of its juices, which is why braising sauces have such great flavour but can leave the meat dry. Braising meat *sous-vide* means that you can control the temperature accurately to 65.5°C—which is high enough to break down the connective tissue and render the meat tender but allows the meat to retain its juices and colour—and cook it for longer. The flavours are intensified and the meat is tender and succulent.

While cooking *sous-vide* is certainly very useful, it should not replace other cooking techniques. I prefer to use it in conjunction with traditional methods. We generally use it to prepare elements of a dish—we may cook a wagyu sirloin in *sous-vide* and then finish it on the grill to get that characteristic smoky flavour of grilled meat, and we will finish white asparagus cooked *sous-vide* in the pan with a knob of butter.

Sous-vide started life as a convenient technique for industrial food production but, as it is used in top kitchens around the world now, it has nothing to do with convenience but is rather about accuracy, consistency and creativity. As cooks, we are always looking for new ways to improve what we do and strive for that elusive perfection. In all the years I have been cooking nothing, so far, has helped us get closer to this goal than the perfection of this technique.

Thoughts about the signature dish

Michel Bourdin, who I worked under when I first started at the Connaught Hotel in London as a young commis chef had a number of favourite sayings, including 'the chef proposes and the customers disposes'. He was a great believer in the restaurant being the star and the diner the ultimate judge. You may create a dish but, no matter how good it is, if it doesn't appeal to your customer base then it is pointless.

It always brings a smile to my face when I read of some unknown young chef who has just written his first menu and proclaims that such and such is his 'signature' dish. It may well be a lovely dish, and it is obviously the one that he is most proud of,

CHILLED VICHYSSOISE, OSCIETRA CAVIAR, BEIGNETS OF OYSTERS

but, until his customers take to it and demand that it never leaves the menu. it has not become a signature dish.

Over the years, each of my many restaurants has had a signature dish or dishes, and obviously these have become synonymous with me. But never have I created something thinking that it will be a signature dish. It is always my guests who have selected it. At Forty One, it was the Crown Roast of Wild Hare with Braised Belgian Endive and Chartreuse Jus, the Oriental Duck Consomme with Duck Sang Choi Bau and the Grilled Sea Scallops, Cauliflower, Tapenade and Green Apple Reduction—they were all created by me and demanded year after year by my diners. Although all those dishes have appeared on my weekly changing degustation menu at the Inn, only one dish has lasted since the original menu. That is the Chilled Vichyssoise, Oscietra Caviar and Beignets of Local Hawkesbury Oysters. After several years of having to include it in the menu, by popular demand, I think we can safely call it the Berowra Waters Inn's first signature dish.

GAME MEAT & OFFAL   189

Crown Roast of Wild Hare, Braised Belgian Endive, Chartreuse Jus

THE HARE

2 wild hares, skinned and gutted

100g (3½oz) butter

sea salt

freshly ground white pepper

CHARTREUSE JUS

bones from the hare

100ml (3½fl oz) green Chartreuse

6 shallots, sliced

1 large field mushroom, sliced

½ leek, sliced

500ml (17½oz) chicken stock

THE ENDIVE

2 heads Belgian endive (whitlof)

20g (⅔oz) butter

40ml (1½fl oz) milk

2tsp sugar

200g (7oz) baby spinach leaves

TO SERVE

pommes puree (see recipe, page 264)

◆ Because wild hare is so lean it should be served rare or medium rare—cooking it any longer spoils the flavour and texture. I recommend a shiraz with this dish.

FOR THE HARE: Remove the front and hind legs from the hare, being careful not to damage the rib cage when removing the front legs. You do not need the hind legs for this dish but you can braise them slowly and serve on another occasion. Save the front legs for the sauce.

Sit the saddle on the board facing away from you. Using a sharp boning knife, make an incision at the top and cut down the side of the spine—do not follow the bone around onto the rib cage as the ribs must remain attached—just cutting deep enough to feel the rib bones. Draw the knife down the side of the spine until clear of the rib cage and then bone all the way through. Now stand the hare on its base and, using a heavy knife or cleaver, chop through the ribs where they attach to the spine, thereby removing the full loin and the ribs intact. Remove the other loin in the same manner.

Once you have all four loins removed, chop the spines for use in the sauce and, using a small 'office knife', carefully clean the skin off each rib and scrape clean until all the ribs are clean of skin and sinew. Using the boning knife, remove the 'silverskin' sinew that lies on top of the loins. You should end up with denuded loins with the clean bones attached.

Lay a loin on a board and, starting at the end without the ribs, roll the loin around itself to end up with a 'crown' of hare. Secure the loin in place with a toothpick or small skewer. Repeat with the other loins.

Preheat the oven to 180°C (350°F). Heat some of the butter in a heavy-based frying pan until foaming. Season the hare with sea salt and white pepper and place in the pan, bone side down so the rib bones splay outwards. Brown the hare loins and then carefully turn them over and brown the bases and then roll them so the sides are browned. Place the loins on a small baking tray with a teaspoon of butter on top and roast in the hot oven for 8 minutes, until cooked to rare. Remove from the oven, lightly sprinkle with sea salt and remove the skewers or toothpicks.

FOR THE CHARTREUSE JUS: Add the hare bones to a stainless steel saucepan with a little olive oil and brown over moderate heat. Remove the bones and set aside. Add the shallots, mushrooms and leek to the pan. When they are lightly browned, put back the bones and add the green Chartreuse. Reduce the liquid by half and then add the chicken stock. Bring to the boil and skim. Simmer very slowly, uncovered, for 2 hours, skimming as necessary. Strain the sauce through a muslin cloth, pour into a clean saucepan and place back on the stove and reduce by half. Whisk in a teaspoon of butter and pass again.

FOR THE ENDIVE: Slice the endives in half lengthways. Heat a teaspoon of butter in a frying pan, add the endives, cut side down, and cook until golden brown. Place the endives in a single layer in a vacuum pouch. Heat the milk and sugar and add the remaining butter; whisk well until emulsified and pour into the pouch with the endive. Seal the pouch and poach the endive in a water bath at 95°C for 1 hour until tender. Remove from the water bath and chill in ice water. Store in the pouch until needed. To reheat, remove the endives from the pouch and drain. Sauté in a little fresh butter with the baby spinach. Season to taste with some sea salt

TO COMPLETE: Warm the pommes puree in a saucepan and spoon some onto the serving plates. Arrange the endive and spinach on the plate. Place the hare crown on the spinach and spoon some of the sauce around the hare.

MAKES 4 SERVINGS

Crown Roast of Wild Hare, Braised Belgian Endive, Chartreuse Jus

Cervena Venison Wellington, Sauce Albufera

Cervena Venison Wellington, Sauce Albufera

THE VENISON

200g (7oz) button mushrooms, minced

50g (1³/₄oz) shallot confit, finely diced
   (see recipe, page 264)

100ml (3¹/₂fl oz) madeira

sea salt

320g (11oz) venison loin, trimmed

20g (²/₃oz) flatleaf parsley, chopped

2tsp chopped tarragon

100g (3¹/₂oz) foie gras lobe, cooked

2 herb crepes (see recipe, page 265)

4 sheets Tunisian brik pastry

1 egg white

SAUCE ALBUFERA

20ml (²/₃oz) madeira

1tsp truffle salsa (see recipe, page 262)

40g (1¹/₂oz) foie gras trimmings

100ml (3¹/₂fl oz) champagne veloute

TO SERVE

200g (7oz) baby spinach leaves

50g (1³/₄oz) butter

8 baby carrots

10g (¹/₃oz) fresh truffle

◆ The venison from New Zealand, known as cervena, has been a great product for many years. In this recipe I have modernised the classic 'beef wellington'. Being a wild game meat, venison is very lean and benefits from this preparation because the meat is protected from direct heat and kept rare. The richness of the foie gras and the mushrooms gives a lovely counterbalance to the gamey meat. The dish is best matched with a pinot noir or even a dolcetto.

FOR THE VENISON: Place the minced mushrooms and shallots in a pan and sweat down. The mushrooms will give off a lot of water—keep cooking until it has evaporated. Add the madeira and reduce again until the liquid has evaporated. Remove from the heat, correct the seasoning with sea salt and add the chopped parsley and tarragon.

Cut the venison into four pieces, season with sea salt and sear in a hot pan on all sides. Remove from the pan and cool. Split each piece of venison in half, not cutting through completely. Open out and place a slice of foie gras lobe in the middle of each slice, then bring the two halves together.

Lay a sheet of clingfilm on a bench. On top lay out a crepe and spread with the mushroom duxelle. Place a piece of venison in the centre and roll up the clingfilm to form a round sausage shape. Repeat with the other pieces of venison, then chill.

Lay out the sheets of brik pastry and brush with egg white. Unwrap the venison and place each piece on a sheet of brik pastry. Roll up the pastries and chill before cooking.

Preheat the oven to 180°C (350°F).

Heat a little butter in a pan and colour the pastries on all sides, then place on a baking tray and put in the hot oven for 10 minutes.

FOR THE SAUCE ALBUFERA: Put the madeira and truffle salsa in a saucepan and heat, then add the foie gras trimmings and veloute and bring to the boil. Blitz with a handheld blender.

TO COMPLETE: Steam the carrots and cook the spinach in butter, then arrange them on serving plates. Slice the venison and place beside the wilted spinach and baby carrots. Spoon some of the sauce around. Finish with some microplaned fresh truffle and truffle slices.

MAKES 4 SERVINGS

Lamb Pot au Feu with Spring Vegetables

STUFFED CABBAGE

2Tbsp shallot confit, finely diced (see recipe,
     page 264)

400g (14 oz) minced lamb neck

1tsp chopped parsley

1tsp chopped chives

1tsp chopped sage

4 large green cabbage leaves,
     blanched whole

THE CONSOMMÉ

100ml (3¹/₂fl oz) egg whites

100g (3¹/₂oz) chicken mince

600ml (20fl oz) brown lamb stock (see
     recipe, page 260)

THE LAMB

1 x 6-bone lamb rack

1 lamb backstrap loin, about 250g (9oz)

2 sprigs lemon thyme

2tsp garlic oil

4 lamb's sweetbreads, prepared (see method,
     page 200)

seasoned flour

100g (3¹/₂oz) butter

50ml (1³/₄fl oz) grapeseed oil

juice of ¹/₂ lemon

sea salt

TO COMPLETE

2 lamb's tongues, poached

8 baby pencil leeks, blanched

4 turned potatoes cooked in brown lamb
     stock (see recipe, page 260)

8 shallots, roasted whole

8 baby carrots, cooked in lamb stock

8 baby turnips, cooked in lamb stock

a little arrowroot

chervil sprigs

long chives

dijon mustard

FOR THE STUFFED CABBAGE: Mix together the shallots, lamb mince and herbs. Lay out the blanched cabbage leaves and, using a cutter, cut out four circles about 6cm (2½in) across. Spoon some of the lamb mixture into the middle of each circle and then wrap the mince, forming a ball. Wrap the cabbage balls in clingfilm and secure with a toothpick or skewer. Keep aside until needed.

FOR THE CONSOMMÉ: In a saucepan, mix together the egg whites and minced chicken. Pour in the cold lamb stock and whisk well. Slowly bring to the boil, stirring occasionally so it does not catch on the bottom of the pan. Once a 'crust' starts forming, stop stirring and allow the solids to slowly form a crust and clarify the stock. Once the stock is clear, pass it through a fine muslin cloth and discard the solids.

FOR THE LAMB: Place the lamb rack and the lamb loin in separate vacuum pouches with the herbs and garlic oil and seal on high. Poach in a water bath at 62°C for 50 minutes. Remove the lamb from the pouches and discard the herbs. Sear the lamb rack in a heavy-based frying pan and then rest in a warm place for 20 minutes.

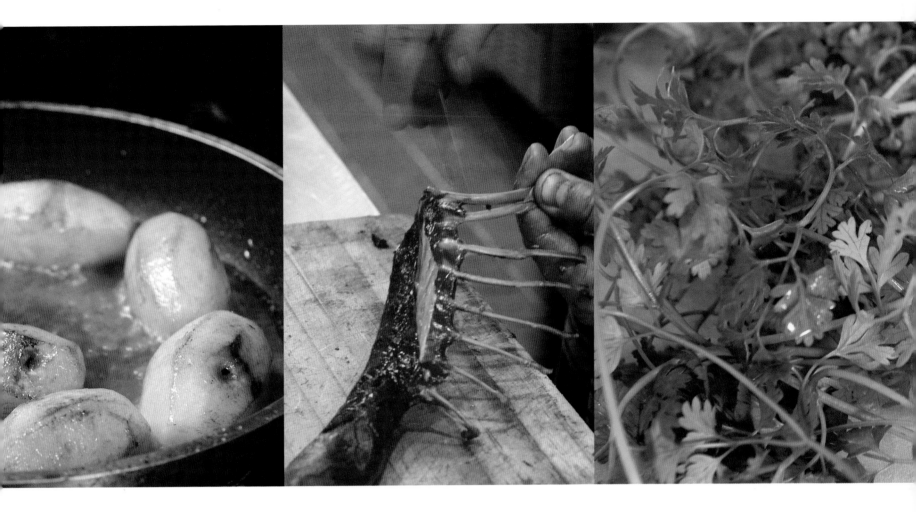

To cook the sweetbreads, first dust them in seasoned flour. Heat half the butter and the grapeseed oil in a heavy-based frying pan. When the butter foams, add the sweetbreads and fry until golden brown, basting them with the butter as they cook. When browned, add the rest of the butter and let it foam around the sweetbreads, squeeze in the lemon juice and season with sea salt.

TO COMPLETE: Bring half the consommé to the boil and add the wrapped cabbage balls. Cook for 5 minutes and then add the poached lamb's tongues and the leeks, potatoes, shallots, carrots and turnips. Simmer gently to reheat all the ingredients.

Reheat the remaining consommé and thicken with a little arrowroot dissolved in water. Drain the cabbage balls, tongues and vegetables from the consommé. Unwrap the cabbage balls. Cut the tongues in half lengthways and arrange in individual serving bowls with the vegetables, cabbage balls and the sliced lamb rack, sweetbreads and loin. Pour over the thickened consommé, garnish with the chervil sprigs and chives and serve with the mustard on the side.

MAKES 4 SERVINGS

Lamb Pot au Feu with Spring Vegetables

Veal Sweetbreads, Langoustine Pastilla, Spinach and Fennel

THE SWEETBREADS

4 x 80g (2½oz) veal sweetbreads (from the
    pancreas)

1 small white onion, sliced

½ leek, sliced

1 carrot, sliced

2 sprigs lemon thyme

500ml (17½oz) water

100ml (3½fl oz) dry white wine

seasoned flour

100ml (3½fl oz) grapeseed oil

100g (3½oz) butter

juice of 1 lemon

sea salt

THE LANGOUSTINE

4 small basil leaves

4 langoustines, peeled and deveined

4 large spinach leaves, blanched and dried

2 large sheets Tunisian brik pastry

1 egg white

50g (1¾oz) butter

SPINACH-FENNEL PUREE

1 medium white onion, sliced

¼ red chilli, sliced

2 small fennel bulbs, sliced

50g (1¾oz) butter

100ml (3½fl oz) Pernod or absinthe

200ml (7fl oz) chicken stock

50ml (1¾fl oz) cream

250g (9oz) frozen leaf spinach, chopped

sea salt

TO SERVE

80ml (2½fl oz) crustacean veloute (see
    recipe, page 261)

FOR THE SWEETBREADS: Place the sweetbreads in a bowl of ice water and soak for a couple of hours, then run cold water over them until there are no more traces of blood. Place the onions, leek, carrot, thyme, water and wine in a non-reactive pan, bring to the boil and simmer for 15 minutes. Add the sweetbreads and blanch for 5 minutes, remove with a slotted spoon and place on a tray lined with a tea towel to cool. The sweetbreads should have firmed up but remain soft in the centre. Cover with a damp cloth and refrigerate until cold. Then peel off any fat, gristle and the thin membrane that is attached.

To cook the sweetbreads, first dust them in seasoned flour. Heat the grapeseed oil and half the butter in a heavy-based frying pan; when the butter foams, add the sweetbreads. Fry until golden brown, basting them with the butter as they cook. When browned, add the rest of the butter and let it foam around the sweetbreads, squeeze in the lemon juice and season with sea salt.

FOR THE LANGOUSTINE: Place a basil leaf on each langoustine tail and then wrap the langoustine in the blanched spinach leaf. Lay out the brik pastry and brush with the egg white. Cut each sheet in half, giving 4 pieces. Wrap a langoustine in each piece, like a small 'spring roll'.

When ready to cook, heat the butter in a heavy-based frying pan. When the butter foams, add the langoustine parcels and cook for 2 minutes, turning the pastries as they brown.

FOR THE SPINACH-FENNEL PUREE: Sweat the sliced onions, chilli and fennel in the butter until soft but not browned. Add the Pernod and then the chicken stock, simmer until the liquid has reduced by half, then add the cream and bring to the boil. Add the frozen spinach and cook until it has melted. Place the mixture in a blender and blitz for three minutes. Pour onto a tray and chill quickly in the freezer compartment of the refrigerator to keep the colour as green as possible. When ready to use, just reheat with a teaspoon of fresh butter. Season with sea salt.

TO COMPLETE: Spoon some spinach-fennel puree onto serving plates and place the sweetbreads on top. Cut the langoustine croustillants in half and stand beside the sweetbreads. Heat the crustacean sauce, then blitz with a handheld blender and spoon over the sweetbreads.

MAKES 4 SERVINGS

Veal Sweetbreads, Langoustine Pastilla, Spinach and Fennel

Grilled Venison Rack, Chorizo-stuffed Medjool Date, Cauliflower Puree

THE VENISON

4 boned venison rack, bones
    cleaned and reserved
1 sprig lemon thyme
2tsp garlic oil
100g (3^1/$_2$oz) garlic butter

THE DATES

8 fresh medjool dates
4 strips pancetta, finely sliced
1 smoked chorizo sausage

80g (2^1/$_2$oz) butter
juice of 1 lemon

TO SERVE

200g (7oz) cauliflower puree (see recipe,
    page 75)
100ml (3^1/$_2$fl oz) beurre noisette (see recipe,
    page 259)
2Tbsp diced tomato
1tsp chives, finely chopped
2tsp micro parsley

◆ I enjoy the sweet and sour contrasts of this dish. The fresh dates with the spiciness of the chorizo and the zing of the lemon work well together and complement the lean rare venison and smooth cauliflower puree. This is best eaten with a pinot noir or even a dolcetto.

FOR THE VENISON: Place the venison rack in a vacuum pouch with the herbs and garlic oil and seal on high. Poach in a water bath at 62°C for 50 minutes. Remove from the pouch and discard the herbs. Sear the vension rack in a heavy-based pan with the garlic butter, then rest in a warm place for 20 minutes.
FOR THE DATES: Split each date down one side and carefully remove the stone. Cut the chorizo into pieces slightly larger than the stone and insert one piece into each date. Reseal the dates and wrap each in a strip of pancetta.
    Heat the butter in a heavy-based frying pan and add the dates wrapped in pancetta. Cook gently, crisping the pancetta all around. Squeeze over the lemon juice.
TO COMPLETE: Heat the cauliflower puree in a saucepan. Reheat the beurre noisette. Slice the venison into four cutlets and arrange on serving plates with a spoonful of the cauliflower puree. Place the warm dates next to the venison. Mix the diced tomato and chives through the beurre noisette and spoon over. Garnish with the micro parsley.

MAKES 4 SERVINGS

CHEESE

Thoughts on cheese

My wife Nicole is firmly of the belief that I am incapable of cooking a meal at home without including cheese in it somewhere. Well, I always say that, being Swiss, they will take my passport away if I do not consume a certain quantity of cheese each year. Joking aside, cheese is one of my favourite ingredients and essential in my pantry.

Cheese comes in so many forms, flavours and textures and its uses are so varied that it can be included in every course of a menu. While I love the cheese chariots that grace the top restaurants of Europe with up to 40 varieties, they are just not practical here. For the cheese course, I have always preferred to list five or six cheeses with individual garnishes selected to highlight the qualities of each particular cheese.

Cheesemaking in Australia has come a long way since I first arrived here. Then, the local cheeses were copies of French, Swiss and English cheeses. It wasn't until the early 1990s that cheesemaking underwent the same revolution the wine industry had gone through several decades earlier and let the local *terroir* show through. Cheesemakers such as Richard Thomas, Gay Kervella and Frank Marchand started making cheeses with real character and quality and that can rank among the best cheeses available anywhere.

This, coupled with the passion of distributors like Simon Johnson, have had a huge impact on Australians' view of cheese as a course in a meal. The next big step is to allow raw milk cheesemaking. Most milk here is collected on a cooperative basis so it makes sense to pasteurise it for consumption, but this disadvantages the cheese industry. Surely there is room for artisan cheeses made from raw milk and industrial cheeses made from pasteurised milk. Raw milk cheeses have got so much more life, depth and layers of flavours and characteristics to them. As soon as you cook milk and pasteurise it by bringing it up to a certain temperature, a lot of its complexity is lost. You effectively denature it: pasteurisation destroys its local characteristics and then all milk effectively becomes the same, as do the cheeses—rather than display the local *terroir*.

Fromart Raclette, Shiitake Mushrooms, Walnuts, Wild Arugula

300g (10oz) raclette cheese from Fromart
100g (3¹/₂oz) shiitake mushrooms
10g (¹/₃oz) unsalted butter
sea salt
40g (1¹/₂oz) salted walnuts (see recipe, page 258)

1tsp red chilli, finely chopped
40g (1¹/₂oz) wild rocket
1tsp shallots, finely diced
2tsp aged balsamic vinegar
30ml (1fl oz) extra virgin olive oil

Preheat the oven to 140°C (275°F). Slice the raclette cheese into four and place each on an ovenproof plate. Place in the warm oven until the cheese melts.

Meanwhile, quarter the shiitake mushrooms, sauté in the butter and season with a little sea salt. When the cheese has melted, remove the plates from the oven and arrange the shiitake mushrooms over the cheese. Sprinkle with salted almonds, chopped chilli and wild rocket dressed with the aged balsamic vinegar and extra virgin olive oil.

MAKES 4 SERVINGS

Gorgonzola Dolce Latte, Saffron-poached Pear, Maple Syrup

POACHED PEARS

50ml (1³/₄fl oz) sauvignon blanc

¹/₂tsp saffron powder

50ml (1³/₄fl oz) water

100g (3¹/₂oz) sugar

1 vanilla pod, split

2 medium pears

TO COMPLETE

240g (8¹/₂oz) gorgonzola dolce latte

40ml (2fl oz) pure maple syrup

4 lemon balm leaves

FOR THE POACHED PEARS: Bring the sauvignon blanc, saffron, water, sugar and scraped vanilla pod to the boil. Peel the pears, halve them and cut out the cores. Place in a vacuum pouch with some of the sauvignon blanc syrup. Seal the pouches in a vacuum machine and poach the pears in a water bath at 85°C for 30 minutes until tender. Remove and plunge the pouch in ice water. Store the pears in the vacuum pouch until needed.

TO COMPLETE: Cut the cheese into four portions and arrange on serving plates. Slice the halved pears and lean against the cheese. Drizzle with maple syrup and garnish with lemon balm leaves.

MAKES 4 SERVINGS

Raw Milk Alpage, Sauvignon Blanc, Poached Apple, Beetroot Oil

POACHED APPLES

50ml (1³/₄fl oz) sauvignon blanc
50ml (1³/₄fl oz) water
100g (3¹/₂oz) sugar
2 medium granny smith apples

TO COMPLETE

240g (8¹/₂oz) raw milk alpage or
   gruyere cheese
40ml (2fl oz) beetroot oil (see recipe,
   page 258)
4 nasturtium leaves

FOR THE POACHED APPLES: Bring the sauvignon blanc, water and sugar to the boil. Peel and core the apples and shape, turning them into small barrel shapes. Place them in a vacuum pouch with some of the sauvignon blanc syrup. Seal the pouches in a vacuum machine and poach the apples in a water bath at 85°C for 30 minutes until tender. Remove and plunge the pouch into ice water. Store the apples in the vacuum pouch until needed.

TO COMPLETE: Cut the cheese into four portions and arrange on serving plates. Brush the beetroot oil across each plate with a brush and arrange the poached apples. Garnish with nasturtium leaves.

MAKES 4 SERVINGS

Livarot Washed Rind, Baby Cabbage Salad, Toasted Cumin

THE CABBAGE SALAD

100g (3¹/₂oz) baby savoy cabbage

sea salt

20ml (²/₃fl oz) verjus

60ml (2fl oz) extra virgin olive oil

15g (¹/₂oz) aged parmigiano reggiano

4 baby kipfler potatoes, cooked in their skins

60g (2oz) butter

sea salt

40g (1¹/₂oz) croutons, fried in butter

TO COMPLETE

240g (8¹/₂oz) livarot washed rind cheese

20ml (²/₃fl oz) lemon-infused extra virgin
   olive oil

1tsp chives, finely chopped

1tsp cumin seeds, toasted

4 red amaranth leaves

FOR THE CABBAGE SALAD: Finely shred the cabbage and season with sea salt. Add the verjus and the extra virgin olive oil and toss well. Leave to stand for 20 minutes. Drain in a colander, then place in a bowl. Grate the parmesan over the cabbage with a fine microplane. Slice the kipfler potatoes and fry in the butter until golden brown, drain and season with sea salt.

TO COMPLETE: Cut the cheese into four portions and arrange on serving plates. Place the sliced warm kipflers next to the cheese and top with a pile of cabbage salad. Drizzle with lemon-infused extra virgin olive oil and sprinkle over the chopped chives, toasted cumin and red amaranth.

MAKES 4 SERVINGS

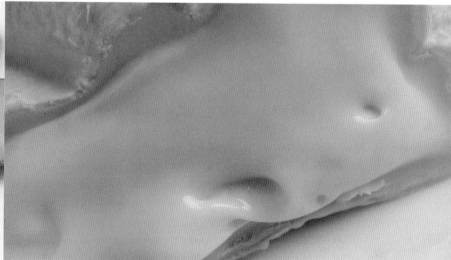

Holy Goat La Luna Goat's Cheese, Balsamic Grilled Fig

GRILLED BALSAMIC FIGS

4 ripe black figs

200ml (7fl oz) balsamic vinegar

100g (3¹/₂oz) caster sugar

1 sprig mint

1 sprig basil

TO COMPLETE

240g (8¹/₂oz) Holy Goat La Luna cheese (or other aged goat's cheese)

4 mint leaves

FOR THE GRILLED BALSAMIC FIGS: Using a pin, prick holes all over the figs and place in a small kilner jar. Heat the balsamic vinegar together with the sugar. When it reaches a simmer, add the mint and basil and pour over the figs. Close the jar and secure tightly. Leave to macerate in the refrigerator for at least 24 hours.

TO COMPLETE: Cut the cheese into four portions and arrange on servings plates. Take the figs out of the syrup and drain. Slice and arrange next to the cheese. Drizzle on some syrup and add a mint leaf.

MAKES 4 SERVINGS

DESSERTS

On chocolate

True connoisseurs prefer dark chocolate, which consists mainly of cocoa bean. The production of quality chocolate is an expensive and time-consuming process and consequently no restaurants make their own, although sometimes we do blend different types and brands of chocolate and adjust the levels of cocoa butter by adding more for specific purposes.

Chocolate is produced by roasting cocoa beans for 30 to 50 minutes at 120–140°C (250–275°F), in a similar manner to roasting coffee beans. Cocoa beans grow in the tropics on the cacao tree—'cacao' refers to the tree and 'cocoa' to the bean after harvesting. Most of the finest cocoa comes from central and south America. After the beans are roasted, their shells are broken open and the seeds, called nibs, are removed and lightly crushed. The crushed nibs from different types of cocoa beans are then blended and ground together between steel rollers, sifted and reground until the powder is in fine particles of around 14 microns. This grinding

is necessary to produce the smooth texture and aromas we desire in good chocolate.

Ground sugar is added to the nibs before heating. The heating forms a paste because the cocoa nibs are around 55 per cent cocoa butter, which melts upon heating. At this stage extra cocoa butter is usually added to give the chocolate better texture—for lower quality chocolate, fats are often substituted at this point rather than the more expensive additional cocoa butter. Although cocoa butter doesn't add so much to the chocolate's taste, it does provide the characteristic texture and helps the chocolate to melt in your mouth.

The cocoa 'mass', or 'liquor' as it is now called, has vanilla added and is 'conched' or mixed. The term 'conch' is derived from the shape of the original mixing machine for chocolate invented in 1874 by Rodolphe Lindt in Switzerland. In basic terms, the longer the chocolate is conched the finer the end quality. Many mass producers only conch for a day, or even less, but the best chocolate makers in

Switzerland, France and Belgium conch for three and up to five days.

The final stage before moulding is tempering the chocolate. In this process, the temperature of the chocolate is raised and lowered to alter the structure of the fat and sugar crystals and make it more stable for use. Tempering makes the chocolate shinier and more brittle. Tempering is lost, however, each time the chocolate is heated, so each time you melt couverture for use you need to retemper it again.

The quality of chocolate is greatly enhanced by the conching and production methods, but its actual taste is determined more by the raw materials: the highest grade cocoa beans from the best plantations produce the very best chocolate. In a lot of ways it is similar to the *terroir* of grapes in the production of wine.

Like all ingredients, you should always use the best you can afford. So what is the best chocolate? As a Swiss, I would like to extol the virtues of Swiss chocolate as the best—and certainly I believe that when it comes to manufactured chocolate bars the Swiss still lead the way in overall general quality. In the professional kitchen it is not so simple. I use a variety of chocolates, depending on the dish we are creating—I'll choose Lindt from Switzerland, Callebaut from Belgium and Cacao Barry from France for general use, but when I create a special chocolate dish I tend to go for Valrhona from France.

Dark chocolate keeps for quite a long time—and some say it even improves as it ages—but it doesn't last forever. It should be protected from humidity

and kept sealed because it will absorb strong flavours from other products. Heat can cause a white bloom on the chocolate's surface but this doesn't actually affect the taste.

On the rise and fall of haute cuisine

Every few years some publication or other sounds the death knell of haute cuisine and fine dining, detailing how the decline in both the desire for and the standards of Michelin-style fine dining, and French cuisine in particular, are dwindling by the passing minute.

True, there are less people who seem to have the time or desire to sit in stuffy ultra-expensive dining rooms and be fawned over by pompous waiters serving overly rich food at stratospheric prices. However, this was what was said when the grand old dining of Escoffier's era was replaced by the fashionable nouvelle cuisine of the 1970s, and then the style of fine dining that endured from then until the beginning of the 1990s.

Inevitably, everything evolves. The new haute cuisine is much more approachable—but haute cuisine nonetheless. Each generation learns from the last and now the disciples of the renowned French chefs Alain Ducasse, Joël Robuchon and others have applied a more modern style to the dining room, resulting in restaurants around the globe serving the same high-quality haute cuisine of the past but in more casual surroundings and, in many cases, at much more approachable prices. As well, the interest in Spanish, Italian and Japanese cuisines has added new flavours and approaches.

But, despite the different influences, the classic French technique is often still the backbone of these modern fine dining restaurants, albeit a technique that has been redefined for the new century. Yes, innovative haute cuisine is more likely to be found in Barcelona than Paris these days but this is a reflection on the French losing the lead in its development rather than the death of haute cuisine. Like everything else in the modern world, haute cuisine is now global.

The very heart of fine dining and haute cuisine is the excellence of produce, the care and love lavished on the cooking and serving of it, and the desire to be the best and to deliver the best to your diners. The wonderful thing is that these days the principles of haute cuisine and fine dining can be found not only at the top end of the market but across the spectrum at different price levels, making it more accessible and not just the privilege of the wealthy.

Haute cuisine is dead ... Long live haute cuisine!

White Chocolate Panna Cotta, Black Olive Caramel, Poached Pear

WHITE CHOCOLATE PANNA COTTA

400ml (14fl oz) cream

1 vanilla pod

100ml (3^1/$_2$fl oz) milk

100g (3^1/$_2$oz) caster sugar

160g (2oz) white chocolate couverture

1 sheet gelatine, titanium-strength

THE POACHED PEARS

50ml (1^3/$_4$fl oz) sauvignon blanc

50ml (1^3/$_4$fl oz) water

100g (3^1/$_2$oz) sugar

1 vanilla pod, split

2 medium pears

THE BLACK OLIVE CARAMEL

200g (7oz) caster sugar

50g (1^3/$_4$oz) liquid glucose

50ml (1^3/$_4$fl oz) warm water

100g (3^1/$_2$oz) pureed black kalmata olives

TO COMPLETE

fresh raspberries

4 sprigs mint

FOR THE WHITE CHOCOLATE PANNA COTTA: Pour the cream into a saucepan, scrape in the seeds from the vanilla pod and add the milk. Drop the vanilla pod in and heat the cream-milk mixture. When nearly boiling, add the sugar and stir to dissolve, then add the white chocolate and stir until melted. Remove from the heat, add the gelatine leaf and stir until dissolved. Pass the mixture through a fine chinoise sieve. Stir occasionally while it is cooling. When the mixture starts to set, pour into 8 x 200ml (7fl oz) dariole moulds and place in the refrigerator overnight.

FOR THE POACHED PEARS: Bring the sauvignon blanc, water, sugar and scraped vanilla pod to the boil. Peel the pears, halve them and cut out the cores. Place them in a vacuum pouch with some of the sauvignon blanc syrup. Seal the pouches and poach the pears in a water bath at 85°C for about 30 minutes, until tender, then plunge the pouch into ice water. Store the pears in the pouch until needed.

FOR THE OLIVE CARAMEL: Warm a pan over a gentle heat and add the sugar and glucose; leave alone until the sugar starts to melt. This will take about 5 minutes—the sugar will have melted and started turning liquid around the edges. Give the pan a good shake and leave until at least half of the sugar has melted. Now, using a wooden spoon, stir the sugar until it has transformed into a dark amber-coloured liquid.

Take the pan off the heat and add the warm water. The caramel will splutter and spit, so do not stand over it. Stir well, add the olive paste and return the pan to the heat to re-melt any lumps. Simmer for a minute, then remove from the stove. Pass the caramel through a fine chinoise sieve into a clean stainless steel bowl and leave to cool. When cold, you may need to add a little hot water to get the right syrup consistency.

TO COMPLETE: Unmould the white chocolate panna cottas and arrange on serving plates with the poached pears sliced into quarters, a drizzle of black olive caramel and a sprig of mint.

MAKES 8 SERVINGS

Braised Pineapple, Coconut Mousse, Semolina Dumpling, Aged Rum Syrup

THE PINEAPPLE

100g (3¹/₂oz) butter, softened

100g (3¹/₂oz) soft brown sugar

2 vanilla pods

1 pineapple, peeled and core removed

THE COCONUT MOUSSE

250g (9oz) boiron coconut puree

25g (³/₄oz) coconut syrup (I use Monin)

40g (1¹/₂oz) icing sugar

175ml (6fl oz) cream

60g (2oz) egg white

25g (³/₄oz) caster sugar

30ml (1fl oz) Malibu coconut liqueur

2¹/₂ sheets gelatine, titanium-strength

THE SEMOLINA DUMPLINGS

125ml (4¹/₂fl oz) aged rum

125ml (4¹/₂fl oz) water

1 vanilla pod

250g (9oz) sugar

250g (9oz) milk powder, full cream

¹/₂tsp baking soda

60g (2oz) plain flour

65g (2oz) semolina flour

30g (1oz) butter, warm and nut brown

milk for dough

grapeseed oil for deep-frying

TO COMPLETE

80g (2¹/₂oz) toasted coconut shavings or
    4 sprigs lemon balm

FOR THE PINEAPPLE: Mix together the butter and brown sugar. Scrape in the vanilla seeds and mix through. Quarter the pineapple lengthways. Put each in a separate pouch with a quarter of the butter mixture. Seal on high. Cook for 60 minutes at 85°C in a water bath. Plunge the pouches into ice water. Keep in the bags.

FOR THE COCONUT MOUSSE: Whisk together the coconut puree, syrup and icing sugar. In a separate bowl, whisk the cream to ribbon stage. In another bowl, whisk the egg whites and caster sugar to stiff peaks, taking care not to overwhip. Dissolve the gelatine in Malibu and add to the coconut mixture. Fold in the whipped cream, then the egg whites. Chill in a clean bowl, covered, in the fridge for 3 hours.

FOR THE SEMOLINA DUMPLINGS: For the syrup, bring the rum, water, split vanilla pod and sugar to the boil and keep warm on low. Brown the butter; mix together the milk powder, baking soda and flours, make a well in the centre and pour in the warm butter and enough milk to make a medium hard dough—it should not be too wet. Roll into balls about 3cm (1in) in diameter. In a deep-fryer, heat some grapeseed oil to about 150°C (300°F) and slip in the balls—they will sink. After a few minutes, they will rise to the surface—they should be be golden on the outside and cooked evenly. As they cook, remove from the oil with a slotted spoon and put in the warm rum syrup. Once all the balls are in the syrup, remove from the heat and leave to macerate overnight.

TO COMPLETE: Reheat the pineapple in the bags in a water bath at 80°C. Arrange the pineapple on plates, with a quenelle of mousse and a dumpling. Garnish with a little toasted coconut or lemon balm.

MAKES 4 SERVINGS

Mandarin and Almond Cake, Mandarin Sorbet, Mandarin Napoleon Ganache

THE MANDARIN CAKE

6 medium mandarins

6 organic eggs

225g (8oz) almond meal

225g (8oz) caster sugar

2tsp baking powder

butter for greasing tin

almond meal for dusting tin

THE MANDARIN SORBET

200ml (7fl oz) mandarin puree or juice

150ml (1¾fl oz) sugar syrup (see recipe, page 266)

2tsp lemon juice

THE MANDARIN NAPOLEON GANACHE

250g (9oz) dark chocolate, chopped

30ml (1fl oz) mandarin napoleon liqueur

50ml (1¾fl oz) cream

TO COMPLETE

icing sugar for dusting

4 sprigs mint

FOR THE MANDARIN CAKE: Wash the mandarins in soapy water and rinse well. Boil the mandarins in water for 75 minutes. Cool, cut in half and remove the seeds.

Preheat the oven to 160°C (325°F). Blend the whole mandarins in the food processor, add the eggs and then the dry ingredients while continuing to blend. Butter 8 x 200ml (7fl oz) dariole moulds and dust with almond meal. Pour in the cake batter and bake for about 20 minutes, until done.

FOR THE MANDARIN SORBET: Mix together the puree, sugar syrup and lemon juice and churn in an ice-cream machine until frozen.

FOR THE GANACHE: Combine the chocolate, liqueur and the cream in a heatproof bowl over a saucepan of simmering water. Stir until the chocolate has melted and the mixture is smooth. Remove from the heat and set aside at room temperature to cool, stirring occasionally until the ganache is firm.

TO COMPLETE: Turn the mandarin cakes out. Scoop out a hole in the bottom of each, hollowing out a third of the cake. Turn over and fill the holes with the chocolate ganache. Dust with icing sugar and serve with a scoop of mandarin sorbet on the side and a sprig of mint.

MAKES 8 SERVINGS

Coffee Parfait, Liquid Caramel, Vanilla Salted Popcorn

250ml (9fl oz) sugar syrup (see recipe,
    page 266)
25ml (³/₄fl oz) coffee essence (I use Trabblit)
6 organic egg yolks
50ml (1³/₄fl oz) Kahlua or Tia Maria liqueur
375ml (13fl oz) thickened cream, whipped to
    soft peaks

THE LIQUID CARAMEL

175g (6oz) caster sugar
1tsp liquid glucose
about 100ml (3¹/₂fl oz) warm water

THE VANILLA SALTED POPCORN

50g (1³/₄oz) butter
100g (3¹/₂oz) popcorn kernels
50ml (1³/₄fl oz) liquid caramel (see above)
1tsp vanilla sea salt

FOR THE COFFEE PARFAIT: Warm the sugar syrup and coffee essence to 40°C (104°F). Place the egg yolks in a heatproof bowl and then whisk in the warm coffee syrup. Place the bowl over a saucepan of warm water on the heat and whisk to form a sabayon. Pour the mixture into a mixer bowl; beat on high speed for 1 minute, then for 4 minutes on medium speed, and then on low speed until the mixture is cool. Add the liqueur and hand-whisk to mix in. Fold in the whipped cream and put the mixture in 6 cone-shaped moulds to freeze.

FOR THE LIQUID CARAMEL: Warm a pan over a gentle heat and add the sugar. Add the glucose and leave alone until the sugar starts to melt. This will take about 5 minutes—the sugar will have melted and started turning liquid around the edges. Give the pan a good shake and leave until at least half of the sugar has melted. Now, using a wooden spoon, stir the sugar until it has transformed into a dark amber-coloured liquid.

Take the pan off the heat and add 50ml (1¾fl oz) of warm water. The caramel will splutter and spit so do not stand over the pan. Stir well, add another 50ml of water and then return the pan to the heat to re-melt any lumps. Pour into a clean stainless steel bowl to cool. When it is cold, you may need to add a little extra hot water to get the right consistency of a syrup.

FOR THE POPCORN: Choose a saucepan with a tight-fitting lid and add the butter. When it has melted, add the popcorn kernels and toss to coat in butter. Put the lid on the pan, increase the heat and 'pop' the corn. When the popping is completed, remove from the heat and add the liquid caramel and season with the vanilla salt.

TO COMPLETE: Unmould the coffee parfaits and arrange on serving plates. Pour over some liquid caramel and serve with the warm vanilla salted popcorn.

Nespresso Granita, Mascarpone Sabayon, Hazelnut Ricotta Cake

THE NESPRESSO GRANITA

500ml (17¹/₂fl oz) nespresso (black pod) strong
   coffee, warm

150g (5oz) sugar

50ml (1³/₄fl oz) Kahlua or Tia Maria liqueur

THE MASCARPONE SABAYON

¹/₂ vanilla pod

200g (7oz) mascarpone

3 organic eggs, separated

65g (2oz) caster sugar

40ml (1¹/₂fl oz) Frangelico liqueur

pinch of salt

THE HAZELNUT RICOTTA CAKE

250g (9oz) butter

250g (9oz) sugar

8 organic eggs, separated

250g (9oz) ground hazelnuts

250g (9oz) ricotta

zest of 5 lemons

65g (2oz) plain flour

pinch of salt

TO COMPLETE

fresh raspberries

◆ This is my version of a deconstructed tira mi su.

FOR THE NESPRESSO GRANITA: Dissolve the sugar in the warm coffee and add Kahlua or Tia Maria. Pour into a tray and place in the freezer. After about an hour, using a fork, stir up the freezing coffee. Repeat this stirring every 30 minutes for 3 hours until frozen coffee crystals are formed. Once the mixture is throroughly frozen, fork it up again and allow the flakes to 'dry' in the freezer for a couple more hours.

FOR THE MASCARPONE SABAYON: Scrape the vanilla seeds onto the mascarpone and beat in, taking care not to overwork. Place the 3 egg yolks, sugar and Frangelico in a bowl, place over a saucepan of warm water on the heat and whisk to a ribbon-stage sabayon. Off the heat, keep whisking until the mixture cools. In a separate bowl, whisk the egg whites with a pinch of salt until they form stiff peaks. Fold the sabayon into the mascarpone, then carefully fold in the whipped egg whites. Store in the fridge until needed.

FOR THE HAZELNUT RICOTTA CAKE: Preheat the oven to 180°C (350°F). Beat together the butter and sugar until light and fluffy. Add the egg yolks one at a time and beat well. In a separate bowl combine gently the hazelnut meal, ricotta and lemon zest. Add the egg-butter mixture to the ricotta mixture with the flour and fold in until well mixed. In a clean bowl, whip the egg whites with a pinch of salt until they form stiff peaks and then fold into the cake mixture. Pour the batter into a 15cm (6in) buttered cake tin or individual tins and bake in the heated oven for around 35 minutes until firm to touch.

TO COMPLETE: For each serving, spoon some granita into a demitasse glass. Spoon some mascarpone sabayon into another glass. Dust the cake with icing sugar and place a slice alongside the two glasses.

MAKES 8 SERVINGS

Lemon and Lime Tart, Candied Eggplant, Basil Gelato

THE SWEET PASTRY

250g (9oz) plain flour

pinch of salt

200g (7oz) butter, diced and softened

100g (3^1/$_2$oz) icing sugar

yolks of 2 organic eggs

1 vanilla bean

egg wash (1 egg yolk and 15ml/^{3}/$_4$fl oz milk)

THE LEMON-LIME FILLING

12 organic eggs

500g (17^1/$_2$oz) caster sugar

400ml (14fl oz) thickened cream

165ml (5^1/$_2$fl oz) lemon juice

100ml (3^1/$_2$fl oz) lime juice

zest of 2 limes

zest of 2 lemons

THE CANDIED EGGPLANT

1 medium eggplant

100ml (3^1/$_2$fl oz) sugar syrup (see recipe, page 266)

THE BASIL GELATO

250ml (9fl oz) sugar syrup

2 basil stalks

zest of 1 lime

500g (17^1/$_2$oz) mascarpone

80ml basil oil (see recipe, page 258)

3tsp micro basil

FOR THE SWEET PASTRY: Sift the flour and the salt together into a bowl or onto the bench. Make a well in the middle and add the butter. Sift the icing sugar over the butter, add the egg yolks and the seeds scraped from the vanilla pod. Using your fingertips, mix the yolks, sugar and butter to form a paste. Gradually draw in the flour and mix to form a smooth dough, taking care not to overwork the dough. If it is too wet, add a little more flour; if too dry, add a little milk. The texture of the dough will vary, depending on your flour. Roll out the pastry between two sheets of silicone or baking paper and refrigerate to rest the dough.

FOR THE LEMON-LIME FILLING: Mix the eggs and the sugar in a bowl and whisk until pale and double in volume. Whip the cream until ribbon stage. Mix the lemon and lime juices and zest into the egg yolk mixture and add the semi-whipped cream. Infuse for a couple of hours in the refrigerator and then pass through a fine chinoise sieve.

TO MAKE THE TART: Preheat the oven to 170°C (340°F). Butter a 20–22cm (8–9in) straight-sided tart ring and put on a baking sheet. Roll out the pastry to 5mm (^{1}/$_4$in) thickness and line the tart ring with it. Leave the pastry overhanging the sides of the ring and make sure there are no holes in the pastry case. Rest in the refrigerator for 15 minutes. Place a layer of greaseproof paper in the tart shell and fill with baking beans. Blind-bake in the hot oven for 15 minutes, and then remove the baking beans and paper. Let the pastry cool slightly, then brush the inside with the egg wash

and return to the oven for 6 minutes until it is lightly coloured. Reduce the oven temperature to 140°C (275°F) and pour the lemon-lime mixture into the tart shell. Return to the oven and bake for 45 minutes until the filling is just set. Remove from the oven and allow to cool and continue to set for a couple of hours before cutting.

FOR THE CANDIED EGGPLANT: Slice the eggplant in half and then into lengths about 2mm (1/8in) thick—this is best done on a mandolin if you have one. Dip the slices in the warm sugar syrup and soak for a couple of minutes. Remove from the syrup and lay on a silicone pastry mat and place in a 90°C (195°F) oven for a couple of hours to dry out.

FOR THE BASIL GELATO: Heat the sugar syrup with the basil stalks. Remove from the heat, add the lime zest and infuse for an hour. Pass the syrup through a sieve. Place the mascarpone in a bowl and gently stir in the sugar syrup, taking care not to overwork otherwise it will become grainy. Pour the mixture into an ice-cream machine and churn. When the mixture is nearly set, slowly add the basil oil while still churning.

TO COMPLETE: Slice the tart and place on serving plates with a quenelle of basil gelato and garnish with the candied eggplant and micro basil.

MAKES 8 SERVINGS

Lemon and Lime Tart, Candied Eggplant, Basil Gelato

Dark Valrhona Chocolate Tart, Sheep's Milk Yoghurt and Almond Cream, Raspberries

Dark Valrhona Chocolate Tart, Sheep's Milk Yoghurt and Almond Cream, Raspberries

THE SWEET PASTRY

250g (9oz) plain flour

pinch of salt

200g (7oz) butter, diced and softened

100g (3^1/$_2$oz) icing sugar

yolks of 2 organic eggs

1 vanilla bean

egg wash (1 egg yolk and 15ml/^{3}/$_4$fl oz milk)

THE CHOCOLATE FILLING

300g (10^1/$_2$oz) dark chocolate (71% cocoa)

200g (7oz) butter

2 whole eggs, plus 2 yolks

60g (2oz) sugar

THE YOGHURT CREAM

20ml (^{2}/$_3$fl oz) almond syrup (I use Monin)

2 gelatine leaves, titanium-strength

100ml (3^1/$_2$fl oz) thickened cream

40g (1^1/$_2$oz) icing sugar

150ml (5fl oz) sheep's milk yoghurt

40g (1^1/$_2$oz) sugared almonds, roughly
   crushed

TO COMPLETE

120ml (^{2}/$_3$fl oz) raspberry coulis

fresh raspberries

mint leaves

◆ This is the classic combination of chocolate and raspberries but I have cut the richness of the chocolate tart by introducing the light sour tones of the yoghurt and almond cream. The best wine match is a Pedro Ximenez sherry.

FOR THE SWEET PASTRY: Sift the flour and the salt together into a bowl or onto the bench. Make a well in the middle and add the butter. Sift the icing sugar over the butter, add the egg yolks and the seeds scraped from the vanilla pod. Using your fingertips, mix the yolks, sugar and butter to form a paste. Gradually draw in the flour and mix to form a smooth dough, taking care not to overwork the dough. If it is too wet, add a little more flour; if too dry, add a little milk. The texture of the dough will vary depending on the flour. Roll out the pastry between two sheets of silicone or baking paper and refrigerate to rest the dough.

FOR THE CHOCOLATE FILLING: Melt the chocolate and butter together in a bain marie. In a heatproof bowl, whisk together the eggs, egg yolks and sugar. Place the bowl over a saucepan of warm water on the heat and whisk to a sabayon. Fold a third of the sabayon into the melted chocolate and mix well. Add the rest of the mixture and combine well.

TO MAKE THE TART: Preheat the oven to 170°C (340°F). Butter a 20–22cm (8–9in) straight-sided tart ring and put on a baking sheet. Roll out the pastry to 5mm (^{1}/$_4$in) thickness and line the tart ring with it. Leave the pastry overhanging the sides of the ring and make sure there are no holes in the pastry case.

Rest in the refrigerator for 15 minutes. Place a layer of greaseproof paper in the tart shell and fill with baking beans. Blind-bake in the hot oven for 15 minutes, and then remove the baking beans and paper. Let the pastry cool slightly, then brush the inside with the egg wash and return to the oven for 6 minutes until it is lightly coloured. Pour in the chocolate mixture and bake for another 15 minutes. When you remove the tart from the oven it will not look set but will firm up as it cools.

FOR THE YOGHURT CREAM: Heat the almond syrup and dissolve the gelatine in it. Whip the thickened cream with the sugar to soft peaks. Add the gelatine-almond syrup to the yoghurt and whisk well to incorporate, then fold in the whipped cream. Store the yoghurt cream, covered, in the refrigerator until needed. Add the crushed sugared almonds about 10 minutes before you serve the cream.

TO COMPLETE: Slice the tart and dust with icing sugar. Place on serving plates with a quenelle of the yoghurt cream. Garnish with raspberry coulis, fresh raspberries and mint leaves.

MAKES 8 SERVINGS

Raspberry Souffle, Raspberry and Mascarpone 'Ripple' Sorbet

RASPBERRY SORBET

500g (17¹/₂oz) fresh raspberries

1 Tbsp honey

100g (3¹/₂oz) sugar

MASCARPONE SORBET

500g (17¹/₂oz) mascarpone

250ml (9fl oz) sugar syrup (see recipe, page 266)

zest of 1 lime

THE SOUFFLÉ BASE

300g (10¹/₂oz) raspberry puree, no seeds

20g (²/₃oz) caster sugar

20g (²/₃oz) cornflour

25ml (³/₄fl oz) raspberry liqueur

THE SOUFFLÉ

300g (10oz) soufflé base (see above)

40g (1¹/₂oz) caster sugar

140g (1¹/₂oz) egg whites

20g (²/₃oz) butter, softened

sugar for moulds.

TO COMPLETE

fresh raspberries

◆ Everybody loves a warm souffle and this recipe is not only easy to make but you can prepare it before your guests arrive, then all you need to do is bake it at the last moment. I love to serve this with a moscato from Italy—if you can get it, the Nivoli Moscato by Michele Chiarlo is my pick.

FOR THE RASPBERRY SORBET: Place the raspberry puree in a blender with the honey and sugar and blitz. Taste and add a little more sugar if needed. Pass through a fine sieve and churn in an ice-cream machine.

FOR THE MASCARPONE SORBET: Place the mascarpone in a bowl and gently stir in the sugar syrup, taking care not to overwork otherwise it will become grainy. Pour into an ice-cream machine and churn. Mix the rasbberry sorbet through the mascarpone sorbet to give a 'ripple' effect.

TO MAKE THE SOUFFLÉ: Make the base by heating the raspberry puree and the sugar in a saucepan. Mix together the cornflour and the raspberry liqueur and add to the boiling raspberry puree. Boil for 2 minutes, then remove from the stove. Pass through a fine sieve and keep aside until needed.

Brush 4 x 6cm (2½in) soufflé moulds with some softened butter and then pour in some caster sugar. Coat the inside of the moulds with sugar and pour off the excess sugar. Whip the egg whites with 40g (1½oz) sugar until stiff, taking care not to overwhip. In another bowl, carefully fold the egg whites into the raspberry base. Fill the soufflé dishes and smooth off the tops. These can be kept at room temperature for up to 3 hours before baking. When ready to bake, place them in an oven at 170°C (340°F) for 10–12 minutes, until risen and firm to the touch.

TO COMPLETE: Serve the hot soufflés with a scoop of raspberry-mascarpone sorbet and raspberries.

MAKES 4 SERVINGS

PETITS FOUR

On the end of a meal

After all that has gone before—the canapés, the savoury dishes, the cheeses and the wonderful desserts—there still remain the petits four. As you sit on its banks, eating delicious course after delicious course, the river flows on beside you—a timeless reminder of the hours passing and the dishes you have feasted on.

There is just a little more before this all becomes a sweet memory, of a long, meandering, wonderful voyage of dishes and delights, on a table by the river in a beautiful glass verandah in the Australian bush. When you think the meal has come to an end, that you have had enough, that you are about to re-enter the everyday, the espresso is served and the waiter appears one more time with a silver tray of petits four to tempt you.

Whether you succumb to the soft flavour-packed fruit jellies or the intense chocolates or the refreshing iced bon bons or a combination of them all, there is always room for one more before it is time to leave.

Pâté de Fruits (Jellies)

900ml (30fl oz) fruit puree

30g (1oz) apple pectin

700g (24½oz) caster sugar

200g (7oz) glucose

2tsp citric acid

150ml (5fl oz) water

granulated sugar

FOR THE JELLIES: Bring the fruit puree to the boil in a non-reactive pan. Mix the pectin and about 50g (1¾oz) of the sugar into the puree and whisk well. Bring back to the boil and add the rest of the sugar and the glucose. Cover and cook until it reaches 107°C (224.6°F).

Meanwhile, mix together the citric acid and the water. When the fruit mixture reaches the correct temperature, remove from the heat and whisk in the citric acid mixture. Pour into a lined tray or moulds and leave to set.

TO COMPLETE: When the jelly is set, turn out of the moulds or remove from tray and cut into desired shapes. Toss in some granulated sugar and serve.

MAKES 4 SERVINGS

Vanilla Kipferl

400g (14oz) plain flour
400g (14oz) ground almonds
170g (6oz) caster sugar

2tsp pure vanilla extract
400g (14oz) cold butter, diced
vanilla sugar for coating

◆ I grew up with these traditional vanilla biscuits and the smell of them baking in the house always meant that Christmas was just around the corner. They are, of course, delicious any time of the year and perfect with coffee and an eau de vie.

Sift the flour and add the almonds, sugar and vanilla essence. Add the diced cold butter and quickly knead into a dough—do not overwork. Wrap in clingfilm and chill for 1 hour in the refrigerator.

Preheat the oven to 180°C (350°F). Take small balls of dough, roll into a sausage shape and then curl to make a 'kipferl' or crescent shape. Place on a greased baking sheet and cook in the heated oven for 7–8 minutes, until golden brown. While still warm, roll in the vanilla sugar and serve.

MAKES 16 PIECES

Iced Chocolate Bon Bons

200g (7oz) your favourite ice cream
300g (10½oz) white chocolate couverture

300g (10½oz) dark chocolate couverture

Using a small scoop, make balls of ice cream and place on a tray to harden in the freezer.

Gently heat the two chocolates over a water bath in two separate bowls. Stick a toothpick into each ice-cream ball, dip in either the white or dark chocolate and return to the freezer to harden. Serve on a bed of dry ice.

MAKES 16 BON BONS

Madeleines

100g (3½oz) clarified butter, plus extra for
    moulds
125g (4½oz) caster sugar
3 organic eggs
250g (9oz) plain flour, plus extra for dusting

1tsp baking powder
zest and juice of 1 lemon
1 vanilla bean, split and seeds scraped out
icing sugar for dusting

Cream the butter and sugar together in a mixing bowl until pale. Add the eggs one at a time and combine until mixed. If the mixture starts to looked curdled, add a little of the flour. Sift the flour and baking powder into the mixture. Add the lemon zest and juice, along with the vanilla seeds, and beat on a low speed in a mixer. Chill for 1 hour.

Preheat the oven to 180°C (350°F). Brush the madeleine moulds with melted butter and dust with a little flour. Place a spoonful of the mixture into each mould and bake for 5 minutes until golden brown. Dust with icing sugar and serve immediately.

MAKES 20 MADELEINES

Dried Sour Cherry and Pistachio Nougat

6 sheets sweet rice paper

400g (14oz) caster sugar

100g (3¹/₂oz) chestnut honey

200g (7oz) liquid glucose

150ml (5fl oz) water

3 organic egg whites (from 55g/2oz eggs)

200g (7oz) split pistachio nuts

150g (5oz) dried sour cherries

◆ Nougat has always been a favourite of mine . The addition of the dried sour cherries counterbalances the sweetness. You need to beat the egg whites while making the syrup.

Line a 20 x 25cm (8 x 10in) tray with clingfilm and cover the bottom with half the sweet rice paper. Combine the sugar, honey, glucose and water and cook slowly. Meanwhile, beat the egg whites in an mixer until almost at stiff-peak stage—do not overmix. When the syrup reaches 140°C (275°F), pour it slowly in a steady stream into the beating egg whites. When it is all incorporated, turn the mixer off and remove the bowl. Using a spatula, fold in the pistachios and dried sour cherries.

Pour the mixture quickly onto the prepared tray and spread evenly. Cover with the remaining sweet rice paper and allow to cool at room temperature. To serve, cut into desired shapes.

MAKES 16 PIECES

BASIC RECIPES

Basil Oil

200g (7oz) fresh basil
400ml (14fl oz) extra virgin olive oil
1 tsp sea salt

Blanch the basil in boiling water for 15 seconds and then refresh in ice water. Drain and dry on a clean kitchen towel. Add the basil to the blender with 100ml (3½fl oz) of oil and start blending to a puree. Add the remaining oil in a drizzle and then add the sea salt. Leave for an hour to infuse. Strain through a muslin cloth or oil filter. Discard the pulp and keep the oil in the refrigerator until needed.

Beetroot Oil

400ml (14fl oz) beetroot juice from raw
    beetroots
80ml (2½fl oz) rice wine vinegar
40ml (2fl oz) extra virgin olive oil

Put the beetroot juice in a stainless steel pan and reduce by half, strain through a fine conical strainer into a clean stainless steel pan and add the rice wine vinegar. Place back on the stove and reduce to around 80ml (2½fl oz). Remove from the heat and whisk in the olive oil. When cold, store in the refrigerator until needed.

Chilli Oil

1 Tbsp Mexican chilli powder
1 Tbsp Japanese mixed chilli powder
1 Tbsp garlic powder
100ml (3½fl oz) apple juice
500ml (17½fl oz) grapeseed oil

Mix together the chilli powders, garlic powder and apple juice to form a paste and then whisk in the grapeseed oil until incorporated. Cover and leave in a cool part of the kitchen for two days, whisking well every 12 hours or so. Strain through an oil filter and store in the refrigerator until needed.

À la greque Marinade

100ml (3½fl oz) champagne vinegar
250ml (9fl oz) chicken stock
100ml (3½fl oz) extra virgin olive oil
juice of 1 lemon
1 sprig lemon thyme
3 whole cloves garlic
1 tsp white peppercorns
1 tsp coriander seeds, crushed
1 tsp sea salt
pinch of saffron powder

Combine all the ingredients in a stainless steel non-reactive saucepan and slowly bring to the simmer. Gently simmer for 15 minutes and remove from the heat. Strain to remove the garlic, peppercorns, lemon thyme and coriander seeds and discard them. Store the marinade in the refrigerator until required.

Salted Walnuts

250g (9oz) good-quality walnut halves
1 Tbsp sea salt
1 egg white
1 tsp extra virgin olive oil

Preheat the oven to 180°C (350°F). Lightly whip the egg white to ribbon stage and then whisk in the sea salt and olive oil. Toss the nuts in the salted egg white and then spread the nuts on a baking sheet. Bake for 10 to 15 minutes, giving them a little toss along the way. Store in an airtight container.

Native Pepper Paste

3tsp minced garlic
150g (5oz) shallots, finely chopped
150g (5oz) fresh ginger, finely chopped
100g (3^1/$_2$oz) native pepper
100g (3^1/$_2$oz) freshly ground black pepper
2tsp sugar
600ml (20fl oz) chicken stock
50ml (1^3/$_4$fl oz) Chinese light soy sauce
100ml (3^1/$_2$fl oz) Chinese dark soy sauce
50ml (1^3/$_4$fl oz) ketjap manis

Sweat the garlic and the shallots with the ginger. Add the native and black peppers and the sugar. Stir well. Add the stock, the two soy sauces and ketjap manis and cook until thickened, around 10 minutes. Remove from the heat and cool. Store in an airtight jar in the fridge for up to a month.

Beignet Batter

200g (7oz) plain flour
200g (7oz) rice flour
1^1/$_2$tsp baking powder
1Tbsp liquid honey
300ml (10oz) vodka
300ml (10oz) lager beer
3 gas chargers for cream whipper

Mix the plain and rice flours with the baking powder. Mix the honey and vodka. Add the vodka mixture to the flour to start making a batter—it will make a sticky dough. Chill overnight. When ready to use, add the lager to make a stiff batter. Load the siphon gun with the batter. Charge with 3 gas chargers. Squeeze the batter from siphon.

Garlic Butter

8 cloves garlic confit (see shallot confit, page 264)
200g (7oz) butter, softened to room
    temperature
1Tbsp chopped flatleaf parsley
1Tbsp chopped chives
1tsp chopped tarragon
1Tbsp chopped chervil
juice of 1 lemon

Puree the garlic in a food processor, add the butter and blend. Add the herbs and lemon juice and mix well, taking care not to overblend. Place the garlic butter in the refrigerator to firm up.

Beurre Noisette

200g (7oz) butter
20ml (^{2}/$_3$fl oz) lemon juice

Put the butter in a stainless steel saucepan and heat gently until a foam is formed. When this foam turns nut brown, add the lemon juice and remove from the heat. Immediately strain through an oil filter to remove the solids and stop the beurre from burning. Either keep warm until needed or chill and keep in a refrigerator.

Verjus Beurre Blanc

200ml (7fl oz) verjus
3 shallots, peeled and sliced
100ml (3^1/$_2$fl oz) double chicken stock
    (see page 260)
50ml (1^3/$_4$fl oz) cream
200g (7oz) chilled butter, diced
sea salt
squeeze of lemon juice

Place the verjus and shallots in a stainless steel saucepan and reduce by half. Add the chicken stock and again reduce by half. Add the cream and bring back to the boil. With the pan still on the heat, whisk in the butter until you have an emulsion. Season to taste with sea salt and lemon juice. Strain and keep warm until needed.

Double Chicken Stock

6kg (13lb) chicken carcasses, chopped
3 sprigs lemon thyme

Make sure the carcasses are well washed and free of blood. Place half the carcasses in a non-reactive stainless steel saucepan and top with cold water. Slowly bring to the boil, skimming off impurities and fat as they rise to the surface. Simmer gently for 2 hours, then strain through a fine chinoise sieve. Put the remaining carcasses in a clean pan, pour the stock over the bones and top up with a little water if necessary to cover the carcasses. Repeat the process, as for the first pan.

After the stock is completed and passed into a clean bowl, leave it to settle for a couple of hours, skimming away any fat that rises to the surface. When cool, place in the fridge. If keeping for longer that two days, freeze the stock.

Brown Lamb Stock

50ml (1³/₄fl oz) grapeseed oil
4kg (8lb 12oz) meaty lamb bones, chopped small
2 large onions, chopped
2 large carrots, chopped
2 cloves garlic
1 large field mushroom, sliced
2L (70fl oz) chicken stock or water
2 sprigs lemon thyme
¹/₂ sprig rosemary

Heat the grapeseed oil in a heavy-based stainless steel saucepan and add the chopped lamb bones. Sauté, browning them well, and remove from the pan. Add the chopped onions,

carrots and garlic and brown well, and then add the sliced mushroom and sauté.

Place the browned bones back on top of the vegetables and cover with stock or water. Bring to the boil and skim off any impurities, fat or sediment that rise to the surface. Add the lemon thyme and rosemary. Simmer for 2 hours, then strain through muslin or a fine sieve.

After the stock is completed and passed into a clean bowl, leave it to settle for a couple of hours as it cools, skimming away any fat that rises to the surface. When cool, place in the fridge. If keeping for longer that two days, I suggest you freeze the stock.

Veal Jus

50ml (1³/₄fl oz) grapeseed oil
1kg (2lb 3oz) veal shoulder, diced
knob of butter
200g (7oz) shallots, sliced
2 large field mushrooms, sliced
150ml (5fl oz) madeira
750ml (26¹/₂fl oz) brown veal stock (made in the same way as the lamb stock, above)
750ml (26¹/₂fl oz) double chicken stock
75g (2¹/₂fl oz) dried porcini mushrooms

Heat the oil in a heavy-based stainless steel saucepan. Add some of the diced meat and brown well—do not overcrowd the pan or it will stew. When nicely browned, remove from the pan and set aside. Add more meat and continue the browning process. When all the meat is browned and removed from the pan, add a knob of butter to the meat fat and fry the shallots until caramelised and then add the sliced mushrooms. Sauté until soft and return the meat to the pan.

Pour in the madeira and add the dried porcini mushrooms, stirring well to dislodge any caramelised meat juices. Reduce the madeira by half and add the two stocks. Bring slowly to the simmer, skimming away any impurities as they rise to the surface. Simmer very slowly for 40 minutes, then remove from the heat and pass through a chinoise strainer lined with muslin cloth into a clean saucepan. Return to the heat and boil to reduce. Keep tasting the jus as it reduces; remove from the heat when it has reached your desired flavour. Pass again through a muslin cloth before using.

Truffle and Madeira Jus

50ml (1³/₄fl oz) truffle juice
100ml (3¹/₂fl oz) madeira
200ml (7fl oz) veal jus (see recipe, above)
50g (1³/₄oz) fresh truffle, sliced or chopped
20g (²/₃oz) butter

In a heavy-based stainless steel pan, reduce the truffle juice and madeira to a syrup, add the veal jus and bring to a simmer. Gently reduce by a third, then add the fresh truffles. Cook for 1 minute, whisk in butter and serve immediately.

Sauce Remoulade

250ml (9fl oz) mayonnaise (see page 263)
100g (3¹/₂oz) cornichons, finely chopped
1Tbsp baby capers, washed and chopped
¹/₂ cup chopped soft herbs (chervil, chives, parsley, tarragon)
squeeze of lemon juice

Put all the ingredients into a bowl and mix together. Adjust the seasoning if needed.

Alternatively, to make a lighter style gribiche vinaigrette, add the garnish ingredients to French vinaigrette (see page 262).

Champagne Veloute

250ml (9fl oz) champagne or sparkling wine
400ml (14fl oz) chicken stock
100g (3¹/₂oz) chopped shallots
100g (3¹/₂oz) chopped leeks
500ml (17¹/₂fl oz) cream
sea salt
freshly ground white pepper

Place the champagne in a non-reactive saucepan, bring to the boil and reduce by two-thirds. Add the chicken stock and chopped shallots and leeks and reduce by three-quarters. Pass through a fine sieve into a clean saucepan, add the cream and reduce by about half. Pass the sauce through a fine sieve again and season to taste with sea salt and pepper.
NOTES: Always use dry champagne or sparkling wine. Variations are done the same way as a beurre blanc—either by adding ingredients to the finished sauce or by varying the reduction.

Crustacean Veloute

600g (20oz) crustacean shells, preferably crab and langoustine
200ml (7fl oz) champagne
50g (1³/₄oz) sliced shallots
50g (1³/₄oz) sliced fennel
50ml (1³/₄fl oz) grapeseed oil
120g (4oz) tomato passata or puree
100ml (3¹/₂fl oz) Pernod
500ml (17¹/₂fl oz) chicken stock
250ml (9fl oz) cream
sea salt
squeeze of lemon juice

Wash the crustacean shells and crush with a rolling pin. Add the champagne, shallots and fennel to a stainless steel pan with the grapeseed oil and reduce the liquid by half. Add the crushed shells and tomato passata and stir well. Add the Pernod and stock and reduce the liquid by half. Add the cream and simmer gently for 30 minutes on the edge of the stove. Remove from the heat and blitz the contents of the pan, shells included, in a blender. Pass the puree through a fine muslin cloth. Chill until needed. When reheating, season with sea salt and lemon juice.

Pepper Veloute

25g (³/₄oz) native pepper paste (see
    page 259)
25g (³/₄oz) sour cream
1 recipe champagne veloute (see
    page 261)

Mix the native pepper paste and sour cream into the champagne veloute with a blender.

Truffle Jelly

100ml (3¹/₂fl oz) madeira
250ml (9fl oz) clear chicken stock or
    consommé
250ml (9fl oz) clear veal stock or
    consommé
50g (1³/₄oz) fresh chopped truffle trimmings
5 leaves gelatine, titanium-strength

Heat the madeira and reduce by three-quarters. Add the two stocks and bring to a simmer, then add the truffle trimmings and simmer for 15 minutes. Pass through a fine muslin and add the gelatine leaves to the warm stock. Stir until dissolved and pass again. Chill to set the jelly.

Truffle Salsa

100g (3¹/₂oz) shallots, finely diced
100ml (3¹/₂fl oz) grapeseed oil

200g (7oz) field mushrooms, minced
100g (3¹/₂oz) fresh truffle trimmings
1tsp tarragon, chopped
50ml (1³/₄fl oz) madeira
sea salt
100ml (3¹/₂fl oz) extra virgin olive oil

Gently stew the shallots in the oil , then add the mushrooms and cook until they have released all their water and are beginning to dry in the pan. Add the truffle trimmings, tarragon and madeira and again cook slowly, uncovered, until the liquid has evaporated. Season with sea salt. Put the mixture in a blender and blitz while drizzling in the olive oil. Cool and store in an airtight container in the refrigerator until needed.

Truffle Vinaigrette

50ml (1³/₄fl oz) red wine vinegar
50ml (1³/₄fl oz) sherry vinegar
100ml (3¹/₂fl oz) truffle jelly stock (without
    gelatine) or veal jus
600ml (20fl oz) grapeseed oil
truffle salsa to taste
juice of ¹/₂ lemon

Place the two vinegars and veal jus in a food processor and blend well. With the motor running, slowly drizzle in the oil. When all is incorporated, add truffle salsa and lemon juice and blitz for a few seconds. Adjust seasoning.

French Vinaigrette

¹/₂tsp Dijon mustard
15ml (¹/₂fl oz) champagne vinegar
1 whole egg
150ml (5fl oz) chicken stock
60ml (2fl oz) grapeseed oil
60ml (2fl oz) extra virgin olive oil

squeeze of lemon juice
sea salt

Place the mustard and vinegar in blender with the egg and blend well. Add the chicken stock and then, with the blender running, add the oils in a drizzle until an emulsion is formed. Adjust the seasoning with lemon juice and sea salt.

Walnut Oil Vinaigrette

2 soft-boiled eggs (2 minutes)
15ml (1/2fl oz) chardonnay vinegar
150ml (5fl oz) chicken stock
60ml (2fl oz) grapeseed oil
60ml (2fl oz) walnut oil
sea salt

Break open the soft-boiled eggs and scoop the insides into a blender. Add the vinegar and stock to the eggs and start blending. Once you have a puree, add the two oils in a steady stream to form an emulsion. Season with sea salt and store in the refrigerator until needed. Shake well before use as this dressing may separate.

Mayonnaise

3 organic egg yolks
1/2tsp Dijon mustard
30ml (1fl oz) white balsamic vinegar
400ml (14fl oz) grapeseed oil
100ml (31/2fl oz) extra virgin olive oil
squeeze of lemon juice

Whisk the egg yolks, mustard and vinegar until pale and double in volume. Add the grapeseed oil in a steady stream, whisking continuously until it is fully incorporated, then add the olive oil. Season to taste with sea salt and lemon juice. If it is too thick, add a little warm water.

Tapenade

80g (21/2oz) field mushrooms, sautéed and chilled
2tsp anchovy fillets, washed
15g (1/2oz) baby capers, washed
1 clove garlic confit (see shallot confit, page 264)
100g (31/2oz) pitted large kalamata olives
20ml (2/3fl oz) extra virgin olive oil

Blend mushrooms, anchovies, capers and garlic to a smooth paste. Add the olives and olive oil and blend again. You may make the tapenade as smooth or as coarse as you prefer.

Brine for Meat and Poultry

2L (70fl oz) water
125g (41/2oz) coarse sea salt
60g (2oz) sugar
6 sprigs lemon thyme
4 cloves garlic
zest and juice of 2 oranges
zest and juice of 2 lemons

Place all ingredients in a non-reactive stainless steel pan and bring to the boil. Simmer for 10 minutes and then remove from the heat. Cool and infuse for several hours. Strain before use and make sure that the brine is chilled before brining the meat and poultry. You can adjust the herbs and flavourings to whatever you wish.

Tomato Chilli Coulis

6 shallots, peeled
40g (11/2oz) butter
1 red chilli, split lengthways
100ml (31/2fl oz) chicken stock
375g (121/2oz) tin chopped plum tomatoes
sea salt

Sweat the shallots in the butter and then add the chilli and chicken stock. Reduce the liquid by half and add the tomatoes. Simmer gently for 30 minutes and then puree in a blender until smooth. Correct seasoning with sea salt.

Shallot Confit

250g (9oz) shallots, finely chopped
1tsp sea salt
enough olive oil to cover
1 sprig lemon thyme

Place the shallots in a stainless steel pan and season with sea salt. Cover with oil and add the lemon thyme. Heat gently and cook slowly, uncovered, until shallots are tender. They can be stored for up to a week in the fridge in their oil. **NOTE:** Garlic confit is made the same way, but keep the cloves whole.

Roast Shallots

16 large shallots
50ml (1³/₄fl oz) grapeseed oil
sea salt
100g (3¹/₂oz) garlic butter (see page xxx)
2 sprigs thyme

Peel the shallots, leaving the roots intact. Brown in the oil in a heavy-based pan. When brown, turn them onto a sheet of foil and season with sea salt, top with garlic butter and thyme sprigs and seal in the foil. Place in a 160°C (325°F) oven and roast for 20 minutes.

Lemon Shallots

24 shallots, peeled
sea salt
250ml (8fl oz) lemon juice
2Tbsp lemon zest
2Tbsp sugar
1Tbsp butter
125ml (4¹/₂fl oz) sauternes
500ml (16fl oz) chicken stock
3 sprigs lemon thyme

Season the shallots with sea salt. Mix together the lemon juice, zest and sugar. Marinate the shallots in the lemon mixture overnight. Drain and reserve the marinade. Sauté the shallots in the butter for a few minutes. Add the marinade, sauternes and chicken stock along with the lemon thyme and cook slowly, uncovered, reducing the liquid until the shallots are cooked and glazed. Chill. Store in the fridge until needed.

Jerusalem Artichoke Puree

500g (17¹/₂oz) Jerusalem artichokes, peeled
sea salt
200ml (7fl oz) chicken stock
200ml (7fl oz) milk
50g (1³/₄oz) butter

Put the artichokes in a stainless steel saucepan, season with sea salt and cover with the stock and milk. Slowly bring to the boil, uncovered, and simmer gently until the artichokes are tender and cooked through, about 15 minutes. Drain the artichokes reserving the liquid. Place them in a blender with the butter and a little of the cooking liquid and blitz, add more of the cooking liquid if needed to make a smooth puree. Adjust seasoning to taste with sea salt.

Pommes Puree

700g (24oz) large potatoes, skin on and
    washed, preferably Sebago
100ml (3¹/₂fl oz) cream
50ml (1³/₄fl oz) milk
70g (2¹/₂oz) cold butter, diced
sea salt

I prefer potatoes baked for pommes puree as
they maintain a better flavour and texture.

Preheat the oven to 180°C (350°F). Prick
the potatoes before putting in the heated oven.
Cook for around 60 to 90 minutes, depending
on their size. Once the potatoes are cooked and
feel soft to squeeze, remove from the oven and
cut in half. Scoop out the flesh with a spoon and
discard the skins. Pass the potato flesh through
a drum sieve or fine mouli if you have one. Bring
the cream and milk to the boil and work it into
the warm sieved potato. Next, add the butter
piece by piece until it is incorporated, season to
taste with sea salt and keep warm until needed.

Pommes Anna

1kg (2lb 3oz) potatoes, peeled, preferably
    desiree
sea salt
100g (3¹/₂oz) butter, melted

Trim potatoes into rectangular-shaped blocks
and then finely slice about 3mm (¹/₈in) thick.
Place in a bowl, season with sea salt and pour
over the melted butter. Toss the potatoes so
they are coated with the butter. Line a loaf tin
with silicone or baking paper. Place a layer of
potatoes in the tin and keep layering until you
have used them all. Cover the pan with foil and
bake in a 200°C (400°F) oven for 30 minutes,
remove the foil and cook for another 40 minutes

or until you can insert a skewer into the potatoes
with no resistance. Remove from the oven and
place a second loaf tin inside the one containing
the potatoes. Put a weight in the second tin and
press the potatoes overnight in the fridge. When
ready to use, turn the pommes anna out and slice
into rectangles. Reheat by frying the stacks in
butter until crisp.

Herb Crepes

12 large organic eggs
250ml (8fl oz) milk
85ml (2¹/₂fl oz) water
125g (4¹/₂oz) plain flour
¹/₄tsp salt
2Tbsp butter, melted, plus 2 or 3tsp for
    coating the pan
20g (²/₃oz) chopped soft herbs (chives,
    chervil, tarragon and parsley)

Whisk together eggs, milk, water, flour, salt
and 2 tablespoons butter until amalgamated—
the batter does not have to be smooth, just
mixed together. Prepare batter at least 1 hour
before cooking. For the best crêpes, let the
batter sit for at least 3 hours.

Before cooking add the herbs. Use 2 or 3
tablespoons of batter for 18cm (7in) crêpes.
Heat the crêpe pan over medium to high heat.
Once hot, coat it with butter or oil. Lift the
pan off the heat as you pour in the batter and,
simultaneously, tilt it in all directions so the
batter quickly covers the surface of the pan.
When the crêpe is almost dry on the top and
golden brown on the edges—about 1 minute
—it is time to turn it. Use a small palette knife to
loosen the edge of the crêpe, then turn it over with
the spatula or your fingers. Cook the crêpe on the
second side, about 15 seconds longer, or until it

is lightly browned underneath. Turn onto a plate. Repeat with remaining batter, stirring it between pourings. Stack the crêpes when cooked.

Braised Pig's Trotters

4 pig's trotters, boned out
1 Tbsp grapeseed oil
2 Tbsp butter
1 Tbsp honey
6 shallots, sliced
1 carrot, sliced
1 leek, sliced
1 clove garlic
200ml (7fl oz) madeira
20g (^{2}/$_3$oz) dried porcini
4L (140fl oz) chicken stock
6 thyme sprigs

Sear the trotters in a heated, heavy-based pan with the oil, butter and honey until a deep golden all around. Remove from the pan and set aside. Add the shallots, carrot, leek and garlic to the pan and fry until golden, then add the Madeira and porcini and cook until the liquid has reduced by three-quarters. Add the stock and gently reduce by half, skimming as required. Place the seared trotters and thyme in the pan, ensuring they are submerged by the stock, cover with foil and braise at 150°C (300°F) for 3 hours. Remove the trotters from the braising liquid and cool. Carefully remove any knuckles or cartilage from the trotters, then layer them between two layers of clingfilm and refrigerate.

Sugar Syrup

250g (9oz) sugar
250ml (9fl oz) water
juice of ^{1}/$_2$ lemon

Place all the ingredients in a stainless steel saucepan and bring to the boil. Once boiled and the sugar is dissolved, remove from the stove and cool.

Folding a Papillote

Lay out the shaped paper and position the filling on one half of the heart shape. Fold the other side of the heart shape over the filling and, starting at the wide end, fold over the edges of the paper in small tucks all the way around, so the parcel is sealed tightly.

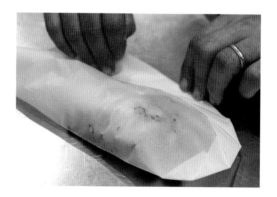

Puff Pastry

225g (8oz) plain flour
^{1}/$_4$tsp sea salt
225g (8oz) butter
125ml (4^1/$_2$fl oz) iced water

Place the flour and salt in a large bowl. Use your fingertips to rub 30g (1oz) of the butter into the flour until it resembles fine breadcrumbs.

Add the water and work gently until a dough forms. Turn the dough onto a lightly floured surface and gently knead until just smooth. Cover with clingfilm and place in the refrigerator for 30 minutes to rest.

Use a lightly floured rolling pin to roll out the dough to a 15 x 25cm (6 x 10in) rectangle. Place the remaining butter between two sheets of clingfilm and tap with a rolling pin to make an 8 x 9cm (3 x 3½in) rectangle. Lay the dough on a lightly floured surface with the short edge closest to you. Remove the clingfilm from the butter and place in the centre of the dough.

Fold the end closest to you over the butter, then fold the opposite end over the top (the butter should be enclosed in the dough) so you have a 15 x 9cm (6 x 3½in) rectangle. Turn the dough 90 degrees clockwise and gently press the edges together. Roll out the dough to a 15 x 25cm (6 x 10in) rectangle and fold over as before. Cover with clingfilm and place in the refrigerator for 30 minutes to rest.

Remove the dough from the fridge and repeat the rolling and folding process four more times. After each, cover with clingfilm and place in the fridge to rest for 30 minutes. In total, the dough should have been folded and rested six times.

Acknowledgements

Having a loving family to go home to at the end of the day makes all the hard work worthwhile … to my darling wife Nicole, who has been my best friend, partner, advisor, assistant and greatest supporter for the last 16 years, a very big thank you for being in my life and making it possible for me to run our restaurants. To my four wonderful children, Dominique, Otto, Pascale and Tobias, of whom I am so proud and are all the lights of my life, and to my parents, Ron and Elma, who taught my brother Marcel and I the love of great food from the earliest age and have always been there when I needed them.

A restaurant's success is due to a great team working hard together to achieve a common goal. Over the years I have been privileged to have many of Sydney's bright young stars come through my kitchens and dining rooms. At the Inn now I would particularly like to thank Rainer Korobacz, my chef de cuisine, who was of enormous assistance with the food photography and, most importantly, does a fantastic job of backing me up in the kitchen on a daily basis; also my sous chef Daniel Backhouse, and the rest of the kitchen brigade, George Kohler, Danial Rudolph, John Fahy and David Bean. Special thanks also to my restaurant manager Tarmara Bower, who has worked with me for many years and guides the service team each week with calm and style, along with her assistant Helen Diab, and to our sommelier Sarah Limacher, who has a wonderful passion for wine and restaurants that is quite infectous.

Also a special thank you to Anthony Flowers, Crosby Mar, Fiona Karpes and Fiona Murphy, all of whom help me make sure that our Ad Lib bistros run smoothly and allow me the time to play at my beloved Inn. It would also be remiss of me not to thank Jeremy and Fiona Laws, who had the vision to let me loose on Berowra Waters Inn in the first place.

No restaurant can maintain its high standards without dedicated suppliers and we have a plethora of them who we have worked with for more years than I care to remember: Anthony Puharich from Vic's Meats, Simon Johnson, Frank from De Costi Seafoods, Steve from Darling Mills Josh from Waimea Trading and to all our many other suppliers of great produce …thank you.

A book is a complex thing to put together and I would like to particularly thank Diane Jardine for her vision for the book and patience in waiting for me to finish it and to the rest of the team at New Holland for breathing life into the book, Mary Trewby and Donnah Dee Luttrell. A special thanks to photographer Graeme Gilles, whose work speaks for itself in the pages of this book, and to Stephanie Souvlis for her invaluable assistance with the styling of the photographs.

Finally, to my valued guests over the many years, a big thank you for supporting my restaurants.

Index

Page numbers in *italics* indicate photographs.

à la greque marinade 258
alpage, raw milk 215
amuse gueule 14–33
    Buffalo Mozzarella, Eggplant Caviar, Tomato
        Chilli Coulis *26*, 27
    Canapé of 'Eggs and Chips' 28, *29*
    Our Duck Proscuitto, Prawn and Celeriac
        Remoulade, Toasted Brazil Nuts 32, *33*
    recipes 24–33
    role of 18–20
    Sugar-cured Salmon, Spiced Avocado, Crisp
        Tortilla 24, *25*
    Tartare of Yellowfin Tuna, Avocado, Asian
        Flavours *30*, 31
apple reduction 75
apple, sauvignon blanc poached 215
asparagus duxelle 159
asparagus
    green 111
    white 154–56
    white, butter-poached 89
avocado 24, 31

Balmain bug dumplings 129
barramundi, fillet of 107–09
basic recipes 256–67
basil gelato 238–39
basil oil 258
beef
    fillet, tartare of *55*
    wagyu 'minute steak' 171
beetroot oil 215, 258
beignet batter 259
Belgian endive, braised 190–91
Berowra Waters Inn, history of 36–37, 78–80,
    118, 137–42
beurre noisette 259
bone marrow dumpling 176–77
Braised Ox Cheek and Grilled Sirloin, Wild
    Mushrooms, Pommes Puree *178*, 179
braised pig's trotters 266
Braised Pineapple, Coconut Mousse, Semolina
    Dumpling, Aged Rum Syrup 230, *231*
brazil nuts 32
brine for meat and poultry 263
brining, on 165
Buffalo Mozzarella, Eggplant Caviar, Tomato
    Chilli Coulis *26*, 27
Buffalo Ricotta Spinach Ravioli, Sage Butter,
    Wood Mushrooms 90, *91*
butcher's meat 162–83
    Braised Ox Cheek and Grilled Sirloin, Wild
        Mushrooms, Pommes Puree *178*, 179
    Lamb Shank, Bone Marrow Dumpling, Baby
        Spinach, Olive Jus *175*, 176–77

    Organic Pork Belly, Lemon-braised Mud
        Crab, Gratinated Pumpkin Puree 172–73,
        174
    Poached Veal Fillet, Langoustine, Leeks,
        Caviar Veloute *182*, 183
    recipes 170–83
    Roast Gippsland Lamb Rack, Sweet Green
        Peas, Wilted Lettuce, Lemon Myrtle 180,
        181
    Wagyu 'Minute Steak', Native Pepper Paste,
        Caramelised Onions, Jerusalem Artichokes
        170, 171
Butter-Poached White Asparagus, Quail Egg
    Croustillant, Watercress *88*, 89

cabbage, baby, salad 216
calamari 103
Canapé of 'Eggs and Chips' 28, *29*
candied eggplant 238–39
caramel, liquid 235
cauliflower 42–45, 103
    puree 75, 205
caviar 50–53, 159
    veloute 183
celeriac 112
    remoulade, prawn and 32
cervena 194–95
Cervena Venison Wellington, Sauce Albufera
    193, 194–95
champagne veloute 261
Chartreuse jus 190–91
cheese 206–19
    Fromart Raclette, Shiitake Mushrooms,
        Walnuts, Wild Arugula *210*, 211
    Gorgonzola Dolce Latte, Saffron-poached
        Pear, Maple Syrup 212, *213*
    Holy Goat La Luna Goat's Cheese, Balsamic
        Grilled Fig *218*, 219
    Livarot Washed Rind, Baby Cabbage Salad,
        Toasted Cumin 216, *217*
    Raw Milk Alpage, Sauvignon Blanc Poached
        Apple, Beetroot Oil *214*, 215
    recipes 210–19
cheese, on 208–09
cherry, dried sour, and pistachio nougat 255
chicken, old-fashioned roast 160
chicken stock, double 260
chicken wings 66–69
    lobster-stuffed 42–45
Chilled Tomato Consommé, Buffalo Mozzarella,
    Basil 126, *127*
Chilled Vichyssoise, Oscietra Caviar, Beignets of
    Hawkesbury Oysters 50–53, *50*, *53*
chilli oil 258
chocolate, on 222–25
    'bon bons', iced 252
    tart, dark valrhona 242–43

    white, panna cotta 228
chorizo-stuffed medjool dates 205
coconut mousse 230
coffee
    granita 236
    parfait 235
Coffee Parfait, Liquid Caramel, Vanilla Salted
    Popcorn *234*, 235
consommé 125, 126
    chilled tomato 126
    oriental duck 125
cooking, on 8–12
couscous, Israeli 66–69
crab croquette 112
Crown Roast of Wild Hare, Braised Belgian
    Endive, Chartreuse Jus 190–91, *192*
crustacean course 56–75
    Grilled Sea Scallops, Cauliflower Puree,
        Tapenade, Apple Reduction *74*, 75
    Israeli Couscous 'Cooked Like a Paella',
        Shellfish, Crisp Chicken Wings 66–69,
        67, *68*
    Mud Crab Mezzaluna, Native Pepper Paste,
        Sweetcorn 72, *73*
    Seared Yamba Prawn Tail, Garlic Butter,
        Parsley, Lemon, Croutons *70*, 71
    Steamed Kangaroo Island Yabbies, Risotto
        alla Milanese *64*, 65
crustacean veloute 261

Dark Valrhona Chocolate Tart, Sheep's Milk
    Yoghurt And Almond Cream, Raspberries
    241, 242–43
dates, medjool, chorizo-stuffed 205
desserts 220–45
    Braised Pineapple, Coconut Mousse,
        Semolina Dumpling, Aged Rum Syrup
        230, *231*
    Coffee Parfait, Liquid Caramel, Vanilla Salted
        Popcorn *234*, 235
    Dark Valrhona Chocolate Tart, Sheep's Milk
        Yoghurt and Almond Cream, Raspberries
        241, 242–43
    Lemon and Lime Tart, Candied Aubergine,
        Basil Gelato 238–39, *240*
    Manadarin and Almond Cake, Manadrin
        Sorbet, Mandarin Napoleon Ganache
        232, *233*
    Nespresso Granita, Mascarpone Sabayon,
        Hazelnut Ricotta Cake 236, *237*
    Raspberry Souffle, Raspberry and Mascarpone
        Sorbet *244*, 245
    recipes 228–45
    White Chocolate Panna Cotta, Black Olive
        Caramel, Poached Pear 228, *229*
dining, on 8–12
Dried Sour Cherry and Pistachio Nougat 255

duck
    breast, seared 150–53
    consommé 125
    proscuitto 32
    sang choi bau 125

eel, smoked 115
eggplant
    candied 238–39
    caviar 27
'eggs and chips' 28

fennel 200–01
fig, grilled balsamic 150–53, 219
Fillet of John Dory, Green Asparagus, Salted
    Grapes, Verjus *110*, 111
Fillet of Murray Cod, Hawkesbury Calamari,
    Cauliflower, Minced Olives *102*, 103
Fillet of Wild Barramundi, 'French Onion Soup'
    Puree, Peppered Oxtail Croustillant *106*,
    107–09
first course 34–55
    Chilled Vichyssoise, Oscietra Caviar,
    Beignets of Hawkesbury Oysters 50–53,
    50, 53
    Galantine of Quail, Foie Gras, Lillet Jelly,
    Toasted Brioche 48, *49*
    recipes 42–55
    Roasted Lobster-stuffed Chicken Wings,
    Cauliflower, Basil 42–45, *44, 45*
    Seared Kangaroo Carpaccio, Warm Kipfler
    Potato, Fresh Winter Truffles *46, 47*
    Tartare of Beef Fillet, Crisp Onion Rings,
    Truffle Jelly, Mushroom Salad *54, 55*
fish, on 100–101
fish course 94–115
    Fillet of John Dory, Green Asparagus, Salted
    Grapes, Verjus *110*, 111
    Fillet of Murray Cod, Hawkesbury Calamari,
    Cauliflower, Minced Olives *102*, 103
    Fillet of Wild Barramundi, 'French Onion
    Soup' Puree, Peppered Oxtail Croustillant
    106, 107–09
    Mulloway Fillet, Crab Croquette, Celeriac,
    Saltwater Pork Belly 112, *113*
    recipes 102–115
    Slow-cooked Ocean Trout, Sweet Green
    Peas, Pig's Trotter, Smoked Eel *114*, 115
    Yellowfin Tuna Pepper Steak, *Pommes Pont
    Neuf* 104, *105*
foie gras 48
    cromesquis 150–53
food and wine matching, on 120–21
food as art, on 58–62
French vinaigrette 262
Fromart Raclette, Shiitake Mushrooms, Walnuts,
    Wild Arugula *210*, 211
fruit jellies 250

Galantine Of Quail, Foie Gras, Lillet Jelly, Toasted
    Brioche 48, *49*
game birds, poultry and 134–61
    Glenloth Squab Baked in Terracotta Clay,
    Winter Truffle Risotto 146–49, *147*
    recipes 146–61
    Roast Organic Chicken, the Old-fashioned
    Way 160, *161*
    Roast Pheasant Breast, Asparagus Duxelle,
    Oysters and Caviar *158*, 159
    Roast Saltwater-soaked Quail, Morels and
    White Asparagus 154–56, *154*
    Seared Duck Breast, Grilled Balsamic Fig,
    Salted Walnuts, Foie Gras *Cromesquis*
    150–53, *153*
game meat and offal 184–205
    Cervena Venison Wellington, Sauce Albufera
    193, 194–95
    Crown Roast of Wild Hare, Braised Belgian
    Endive, Chartreuse Jus 190–91, *192*
    Grilled Vension Rack, Chorizo-stuffed
    Medjool Date, Cauliflower Puree *204*, 205
    Lamb Pot au Feu with Spring Vegetables
    196–97, *198–99*
    recipes 190–205
    Veal Sweetbreads, Langoustine Pastilla,
    Spinach and Fennel 200–01, *203*
garlic butter 71, 259
Glenloth Squab Baked in Terracotta Clay, Winter
    Truffle Risotto 146–49, *147*
goat's cheese 219
    fondue 85
gorgonzola dolce latte 212
Gorgonzola Dolce Latte, Saffron-Poached Pear,
    Maple Syrup 212, *213*
grapes, salted 111
Grilled Sea Scallops, Cauliflower Puree, Tapenade,
    Apple Reduction 74, *75*
Grilled Vension Rack, Chorizo-stuffed Medjool
    Date, Cauliflower Puree *204*, 205

hare, crown roast of wild 190–91
haute cuisine, on the rise and fall of 225–26
hazelnut ricotta cake 236
herb crêpes 265
Holy Goat La Luna Goat's Cheese, Balsamic
    Grilled Fig *218*, 219

Iced Chocolate 'Bon Bons' 252, *253*
Israeli Couscous 'Cooked Like a Paella', Shellfish,
    Crisp Chicken Wings 66–69, *67*, 68

Jerusalem artichoke
    fondants 171
    puree 264
john dory, fillet of 111

kangaroo carpaccio, seared 47
kipferl, vanilla 251

Lamb Pot au Feu with Spring Vegetables 196–97,
    198–99
lamb rack, roast 180
lamb shank 176–77
Lamb Shank, Bone Marrow Dumpling, Baby
    Spinach, Olive Jus *175*, 176–77
lamb stock, brown 260
langoustine 183
    pastilla 200–01
leeks 130, 183
lemon and lime tart 238–39
Lemon and Lime Tart, Candied Eggplant, Basil
    Gelato 238–39, *240*
lemon shallots 264
    tart tatin of 85
lettuce, wilted 180
Lillet jelly 48
livarot washed rind 216
Livarot Washed Rind, Baby Cabbage Salad,
    Toasted Cumin 216, *217*
lobster-stuffed chicken wings 42–45

Madeleines 254, *254*
Manadarin and Almond Cake, Manadrin Sorbet,
    Mandarin Napoleon Ganache 232, *233*
manadrin sorbet 232
mandarin napoleon ganache 232
mascarpone sabayon 236
mayonnaise 263
meal, on the end of 248
meat, *see* butcher's, game meat and offal
meat brine 263
menu, importance of 20–23
mise en place, importance of 38–39
mozzarella, buffalo 27, 126
mud crab
    lemon-braised 172–73
    mezzaluna 72
Mud Crab Mezzaluna, Native Pepper Paste,
    Sweetcorn 72, *73*
Mulloway Fillet, Crab Croquette, Celeriac,
    Saltwater Pork Belly 112, *113*
murray cod, fillet of 103
mushroom salad 55
mushrooms 90, 93
    morels 154–56
    shiitake 211
    wild 179

native pepper paste 72, 171, 259
Nespresso Granita, Mascarpone Sabayon,
    Hazelnut Ricotta Cake 236, *237*

ocean trout, slow-cooked 115
offal, game meat and 184–205
    Cervena Venison Wellington, Sauce Albufera
    193, 194–95
    Crown Roast of Wild Hare, Braised Belgian
    Endive, Chartreuse Jus 190–91, *192*
    Grilled Vension Rack, Chorizo-stuffed

Medjool Date, Cauliflower Puree 204, 205
Lamb Pot au Feu with Spring Vegetables
   196–97, 198–99
recipes 190–205
Veal Sweetbreads, Langoustine Pastilla,
   Spinach and Fennel 200–01, 203
olive
   caramel 228
   jus 176–77
olives 103
onion rings, 55
onion soup puree, French 107–09
onions, caramelised 171
Organic Pork Belly, Lemon-Braised Mud Crab,
   Gratinated Pumpkin Puree 172–73, 174
Oriental Duck Consommé, Roast Duck Sang
   Choi Bau 124, 125
Our Duck Proscuitto, Prawn and Celeriac
   Remoulade, Toasted Brazil Nuts 32, 33
ox cheek, braised, and grilled sirloin 179
oxtail croustillant, peppered 107–09
oysters 159
   beignets of Hawkesbury 50–53

panna cotta, white chocolate 228
papillote, folding 266
Pâté des Fruits 250, 250
pear, poached 228
pear, saffron-poached 212
peas 115, 130, 180
pecorino 130
pepper veloute 262
petits four 246–55
   Dried Sour Cherry and Pistachio Nougat
     255, 255
   Iced Chocolate 'Bon Bons' 252, 253
   Madeleines 254, 254
   Pâté des Fruits 250, 250
   recipes 250–55
   Vanilla Kipferl 251, 251
pheasant breast, roast 159
pig's trotter 115, 266
pineapple, braised 230
pistachio and dried sour cherry nougat 255
Poached Veal Fillet, Langoustine, Leeks, Caviar
   Veloute 182, 183
pommes anna 265
pommes pont neuf 104
pommes puree 179, 265
popcorn, vanilla salted 235
pork belly 112, 172–73
pot au feu 196–97
potato 130
   pommes anna 265
   pommes pont neuf 104
   pommes puree 179, 265
   warm kipfler 47
potato, leek and truffle soup 132, 133
poultry and game birds 134–61

Glenloth Squab Baked in Terracotta Clay,
   Winter Truffle Risotto 146–49, 147
recipes 146–61
Roast Organic Chicken, the Old-fashioned
   Way 160, 161
Roast Pheasant Breast, Asparagus Duxelle,
   Oysters and Caviar 158, 159
Roast Saltwater-soaked Quail, Morels and
   White Asparagus 154–56, 154
Seared Duck Breast, Grilled Balsamic Fig,
   Salted Walnuts, Foie Gras Cromesquis
   150–53, 153
poultry brine 263
prawn and celeriac remoulade 32
prawn tail, seared yamba 71
prosciutto 130
   duck 32
puff pastry 266
pumpkin puree, gratinated 172–73

quail
   galantine of 48
   roast saltwater-soaked 154–56
quail egg croustillant 89

raclette, Fromart 211
raspberries 242–43
raspberry
   and mascarpone sorbet 245
   souffle 245
Raspberry Souffle, Raspberry and Mascarpone
   Sorbet 244, 245
ravioli, buffalo ricotta spinach 90
Raw Milk Alpage, Sauvignon Blanc Poached
   Apple, Beetroot Oil 214, 215
recipes, using 12–13
remote restaurants, on 39–40
restaurant
   on how to use a good 96–100
   on successful 16–18
   remote, on 39–40
   reservations, on 80–83
   reviewers, on 165–69
risotto
   alla milanese 65
   winter truffle 146–49
Roast Gippsland Lamb Rack, Sweet Green Peas,
   Wilted Lettuce, Lemon Myrtle 180, 181
Roast Organic Chicken, the Old-fashioned Way
   160, 161
Roast Pheasant Breast, Asparagus Duxelle, Oysters
   and Caviar 158, 159
Roast Saltwater-Soaked Quail, Morels and White
   Asparagus 154–56, 154
roast shallots 264
Roasted Lobster-stuffed Chicken Wings,
   Cauliflower, Basil 42–45, 44, 45

sage butter 90
salmon 24

salted
   grapes 111
   walnuts 150–53, 258
sauce albufera 194–95
sauce remoulade 261
scallops, grilled 75
Seared Duck Breast, Grilled Balsamic Fig, Salted
   Walnuts, Foie Gras Cromesquis 150–53, 153
Seared Kangaroo Carpaccio, Warm Kipfler
   Potato, Fresh Winter Truffles 46, 47
Seared Yamba Prawn Tail, Garlic Butter, Parsley,
   Lemon, Croutons 70, 71
semolina dumpling 230
shallot confit 264
shallots, roast 264
shellfish 66–69
   on 62–63
   see crustacean course
signature dish, on the 188–89
sirloin, grilled, and braised ox cheek 179
Slow-Cooked Ocean Trout, Sweet Green Peas,
   Pig's Trotter, Smoked Eel 114, 115
soup, on 121–23
soup course 116–33
   Chilled Tomato Consommé, Buffalo
     Mozzarella, Basil 126, 127
   Oriental Duck Consommé, Roast Duck Sang
     Choi Bau 124, 125
   Potato, Leek and Truffle Soup 132, 133
   recipes 125–33
   Sweetcorn Veloute, Balmain Bug Dumplings
     128, 129
   Yabbie Bisque, Crushed Peas, Pecorino,
     Prosciutto, Basil, Mint 130, 131
sous-vide, on 186–88
spaetzli noodles 86
Spaetzli Noodles, Organic Egg Yolk, Baby
   Spinach, Fresh Winter Truffles 86, 87
spaghettini 'en papilotte' 93
Spaghettini 'En Papilotte' with Rocket, Wild
   Mushrooms, Garlic and Chilli Oil 92, 93
spinach 86, 176–77, 200–01
squab baked in terracotta clay 146–49
Steamed Kangaroo Island Yabbies, Risotto alla
   Milanese 64, 65
sugar syrup 266
sweetcorn 72
   veloute 129
Sweetcorn Veloute, Balmain Bug Dumplings 128,
   129
syrup, aged rum 230

tapenade 75, 263
Tart Tatin of Lemon Shallots, Goat's Cheese
   Fondue, Wild Rocket 84, 85
Tartare of Beef Fillet, Crisp Onion Rings, Truffle
   Jelly, Mushroom Salad 54, 55
Tartare of Yellowfin Tuna, Avocado, Asian Flavours
   30, 31

tomato chilli coulis 27, 263
tomato consommé, chilled 126
tools of the trade, on 143–45
tortilla 24
truffle
    and madeira jus 261
    in risotto 146–49
    in soup 133
    jelly 55, 262
    salsa 262
    vinaigrette 262
truffles 47, 86
tuna, yellowfin 31, 104

Vanilla Kipferl 251, 251
veal fillet, poached 183
veal jus 260
veal sweetbreads 200–01
Veal Sweetbreads, Langoustine Pastilla, Spinach

and Fennel 200–01, 203
vegetable course 76–93
    Buffalo Ricotta Spinach Ravioli, Sage Butter,
        Wood Mushrooms 90, 91
    Butter-poached White Asparagus, Quail Egg
        Croustillant, Watercress 88, 89
    recipes 84–93
    Spaetzli Noodles, Organic Egg Yolk, Baby
        Spinach, Fresh Winter Truffles 86, 87
    Spaghettini 'En Papilotte' with Rocket, Wild
        Mushrooms, Garlic and Chilli Oil 92, 93
    Tart Tatin of Lemon Shallots, Goat's Cheese
        Fondue, Wild Rocket 84, 85
vegetables, spring 196–97
venison wellington 194–95
vension rack, grilled 205
verjus 111
    beurre blanc 259
vichyssoise, chilled 50–53

Wagyu 'Minute Steak', Native Pepper Paste,
    Caramelised Onions, Jerusalem Artichokes
    170, 171
waiters, on the care and training of 136–37
walnut oil vinaigrette 263
walnuts 211
    salted 150–53, 258
White Chocolate Panna Cotta, Black Olive
    Caramel, Poached Pear 228, 229
wild rocket 85, 211
witlof, braised 190–91

yabbie bisque 130
Yabbie Bisque, Crushed Peas, Pecorino,
    Prosciutto, Basil, Mint 130, 131
yabbies, steamed kangaroo island 65
Yellowfin Tuna Pepper Steak, Pommes Pont
    Neuf 104, 105
yoghurt, sheep's milk, and almond cream 242–43

First published in 2010 by New Holland Publishers (Australia) Pty Ltd
Sydney • Auckland • London • Cape Town

www.newholland.com.au

1/66 Gibbes Street Chatswood NSW 2067 Australia
218 Lake Road Northcote Auckland New Zealand
86 Edgware Road London W2 2EA United Kingdom
80 McKenzie Street Cape Town 8001 South Africa

Copyright © 2010 in text: Dietmar Sawyere
Copyright © 2010 in images: Graeme Gillies/NHIL
Copyright © 2010 New Holland Publishers (Australia) Pty Ltd

A record of this book is available at the National Library of Australia

ISBN 9781741108699

Publisher: Diane Jardine
Editor: Mary Trewby
Cover and internal design: Donnah Dee Luttrell
Photography: Graeme Gillies
Stylist: Stephanie Souvlis
Publishing manager: Lliane Clarke
Production manager: Olga Dementiev
Printer: Toppan Leefung Printing Limited (China)